History of Empires

An Enthralling Journey through the Rise and Fall of Dominant Powers across the Ages

© Copyright 2025 - All rights reserved.

The content contained within this book may not be reproduced, duplicated, or transmitted without direct written permission from the author or the publisher.

Under no circumstances will any blame or legal responsibility be held against the publisher, or author, for any damages, reparation, or monetary loss due to the information contained within this book, either directly or indirectly.

Legal Notice:

This book is copyright protected. It is only for personal use. You cannot amend, distribute, sell, use, quote, or paraphrase any part, or the content within this book, without the consent of the author or publisher.

Disclaimer Notice:

Please note the information contained within this document is for educational and entertainment purposes only. All effort has been executed to present accurate, up-to-date, reliable, and complete information. No warranties of any kind are declared or implied. Readers acknowledge that the author is not engaging in the rendering of legal, financial, medical, or professional advice. The content within this book has been derived from various sources. Please consult a licensed professional before attempting any techniques outlined in this book.

By reading this document, the reader agrees that under no circumstances is the author responsible for any losses, direct or indirect, that are incurred as a result of the use of the information contained within this document, including, but not limited to, errors, omissions, or inaccuracies.

Free limited time bonus

Stop for a moment. We have a free bonus set up for you. The problem is this: we forget 90% of everything that we read after 7 days. Crazy fact, right? Here's the solution: we've created a printable, 1-page pdf summary for this book that you're reading now. All you have to do to get your free pdf summary is to go to the following website:
https://livetolearn.lpages.co/enthrallinghistory/

Or, Scan the QR code!

Once you do, it will be intuitive. Enjoy, and thank you!

Table of Contents

INTRODUCTION 1
CHAPTER 1: SARGON THE GREAT AND MESOPOTAMIA 3
CHAPTER 2: THE GREAT WALL AND THE QIN DYNASTY 16
CHAPTER 3: THE END OF THE ROMAN REPUBLIC 28
CHAPTER 4: CLEOPATRA'S EGYPT 40
CHAPTER 5: GENGHIS KHAN AND THE MONGOL EMPIRE 53
CHAPTER 6: THE AZTEC EMPIRE 66
CHAPTER 7: THE BRITISH EMPIRE 78
CHAPTER 8: THE FRENCH REVOLUTION AND THE DAWN OF
A NEW ERA 89
CHAPTER 9: THE RISE AND FALL OF THE SOVIET UNION 99
CONCLUSION 110
HERE'S ANOTHER BOOK BY ENTHRALLING HISTORY THAT
YOU MIGHT LIKE 112
FREE LIMITED TIME BONUS 113
BIBLIOGRAPHY 114
IMAGE SOURCES 117

Introduction

Ur-Zababa, king of Kish, paced back and forth in a rage. "That Sargon! Who is he? Nothing more than the gardener's son! Not even that—he's a foundling! No one knows where he's really from. And now, the goddess Inanna is showering her favor on him. All the gods are against me! That's the thanks I get for making a nobody my cupbearer. Now, I've got to get rid of him before he usurps my throne! What to do?"

Ur-Zababa scowled as he smoothed his long beard. Suddenly, he clapped his hands, his face beaming. "I know! I'll have my metalsmith push him into a statue mold and pour molten bronze over him. Sargon will become my new bronze statue!" Ur-Zababa almost leaped for joy as he rubbed his hands together. "Ha! I'll even build a little temple for my new statue. No one will know it's really Sargon."

Unfortunately for Ur-Zababa, his plot fell through. Sargon survived and went on to establish the world's first empire in what is today's Iraq.

An empire is a group of countries or states governed by one ruler. It usually includes multiple language groups and ethnicities but has a strong central government. Many empires have risen and fallen around the globe since Sargon's Akkadian Empire. This book explores the compelling stories of some of history's most pivotal empires. How did they change the world? Why did they rise to greatness, only to come crashing down? Who were the key figures, and what made them exceptional? How did life-changing events define their trajectory? What were the cultural dynamics and the human stories?

Diving into the histories of our planet's extraordinary empires helps us understand our world today. How did we get where we are now? What were the watershed moments along the way? How did ancient cultures influence our beliefs and worldviews today? What are the inspirational and motivational stories from these empires? Do they warn us of what *not* to do?

This book will not bore you with lists of dates and dry facts. It is full of spellbinding stories of the fascinating men and women who built empires and others who tore them down. It is the tale of winners and losers who changed the world. Some were ingenious role models, others were diabolically destructive, yet they all set the stage for today's world. Unwrapping the histories of these empires around the globe helps us understand today's turbulent political landscape. Let's travel around the world and unlock their legacies.

Chapter 1: Sargon the Great and Mesopotamia

Tales of baby boys in baskets floating down rivers appear in several ancient cultures. The Nile carried the baby Moses along until the pharaoh's daughter rescued him. Romulus and Remus sailed down the Tiber River to be suckled by a she-wolf. Yet long before the founders of Israel and Rome, a baby floated down the Euphrates River in ancient Iraq, according to the *Legend of Sargon of Akkadê*:

> Sargon, the mighty king, king of Agade, am I... My mother conceived me in secret; she gave birth to me in concealment. She set me in a basket of rushes; she sealed my lid with bitumen. She cast me into the river, but it did not rise over me.
>
> The water carried me to Akki, the drawer of water. He lifted me out as he dipped his jar into the river. Akki took me as his son; he raised me and made me his gardener. While I was a gardener, (the goddess) Ishtar granted me her love.[i]

Almost 1,700 years later, the Neo-Assyrians placed Sargon's story, inscribed on clay tablets, in the Library of Ashurbanipal at Nineveh, the capital of their empire. The ancient library held texts the Assyrians collected while raiding other civilizations. Were these tablets copies of

---

[i] *The Legend of Sargon of Akkadê, c. 2300 BCE* (Fordham University, Internet Ancient History Sourcebook, 1999). https://sourcebooks.fordham.edu/ancient/2300sargon1.asp.

what Sargon himself wrote about his origins? No one knows, although most historians think someone else wrote his story much later.

Before Sargon arrived on the scene, what was ancient Iraq's political, social, and cultural landscape? What great civilizations had already left their mark on the region? How did Sargon unite these cultures to form the world's first empire?

Weirdly, although most people have heard of the Babylonian and Assyrian empires that came later, many people are not familiar with Sargon's Akkadian Empire, the first in the world. This chapter aims to correct that!

Why Is Ancient Mesopotamia Called the "Cradle of Civilization"?

The ancient Greeks gave the name "Mesopotamia" to the region that includes today's Iraq and parts of Iran, Kuwait, Saudi Arabia, Syria, and Turkey. Mesopotamia means "between the rivers," as its most important region lay between the Euphrates and Tigris rivers. These two rivers that emptied into the Persian Gulf made Mesopotamia the ancient world's key trade hub.

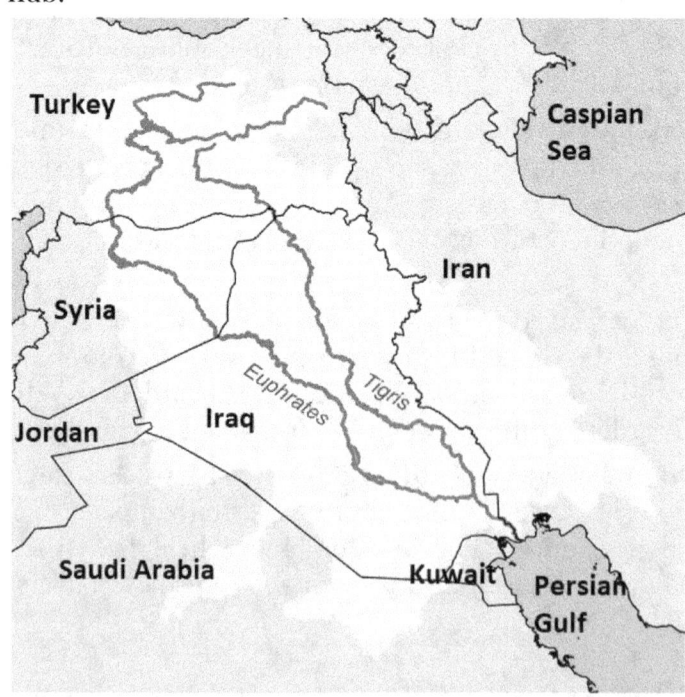

Mesopotamia was the light area on this modern map of the Middle East.[1]

Mesopotamia is called the "cradle of civilization" because its history is an awe-inspiring account of beginnings. The Mesopotamians produced an astounding number of innovations. Around 6000 BCE, the Hassuna, Samarra, Halaf, and Ubaid civilizations emerged in ancient Iraq. They herded cattle, goats, and sheep and built sun-dried brick houses. They began cultivating the land with simple plows to grow barley, flax, emmer wheat, and lentils. Using stone mortars, these ancient people ground the grains into flour to make dough. They baked the dough in clay ovens like the *tannūr* (tandoor) ovens still used today in the Middle East and Indian subcontinent.

The Ubaid people built Eridu around 5400 BCE near the Persian Gulf. The ancient *Sumerian King List* says it was the first city (and it most likely was). Eridu covered twenty-five acres, and its population grew to about four thousand people. It had a temple, infrastructure, a central government, and irrigation canals that watered the farmland around the city. The Ubaid burial grounds had small models of the masted reed sailboats they used to navigate the Persian Gulf.

The Ubaid also built the towns of Ur and Uruk around 5000 BCE. They abandoned Ur and Eridu around 3700 BCE when climate change brought desertification. Uruk was on the Euphrates River, so it survived with a steady water source. The Sumerian people rebuilt Ur and Eridu several centuries later when the climate became more favorable. Ur was the childhood home of the patriarch Abraham during the late Akkadian Empire.

The Sumerians, who called themselves the "black-haired people," may have been a remnant of the Ubaid people or a new civilization that migrated into southern Mesopotamia. They rebuilt the Ubaid cities and made stunning innovations. The Sumerians introduced the world to the first writing system by 3500 BCE. They used reeds to scratch tiny pictures (pictographs) into soft clay that hardened into tablets. Over time, the pictographs became abstract wedge-shaped glyphs in a system known as cuneiform writing. Thankfully, thousands of cuneiform clay tablets survived to the present day, revealing incredible insight into ancient cultures, including the Akkadians, Assyrians, Babylonians, Elamites, and Hittites.

The world's first known wheel was a potter's wheel invented in Iran by 5200 BCE. The Sumerians took it to the next level around 3750 BCE by inventing the axle and building wheeled carts pulled by donkeys. Before long, soldiers rode to war in four-wheeled chariots. The time measurements we use today—the twelve-hour day, the sixty-minute hour, and the sixty-second minute—all came from the Sumerians. By 2600 BCE, the Sumerians developed multiplication, division, cubic and square roots, and simple geometry.

A decorative box crafted around 2600 BCE pictures this early chariot.[2]

By the time Akki, the palace gardener, pulled the baby Sargon from the river, various Sumerian city-states (a large, strong city and its surrounding villages and towns) had become powerful enough to conquer and rule neighboring city-states. These were not true empires because everyone shared the same culture and language.

By 3000 BCE, Semitic-speaking shepherds migrated in from Syria and settled throughout Mesopotamia, mostly in the north. One group was the Akkadians, whose language traces them to Ebla in ancient Syria. Ebla was a trade partner with the city of Kish in Sumer, where Sargon grew up.

The Akkadian language later evolved into the Assyrian and Babylonian dialects. The Akkadians settled Agade (Akkad), which later became Sargon's capital. Agade's location is a mystery. All we know is that it was on the Tigris River. It lies hidden somewhere under the blowing desert sands.

What Are the Legends of Sargon's Origins and Early Life?

The *Sumerian King List*, written in the late third millennium BCE, says that after the Great Flood, the first city to hold "kingship" was Kish, about fifty miles south of today's Baghdad.[i] "Kingship" meant that a city-state dominated other cities. Over the centuries, kingship shifted to Eridu, Ur, Uruk, and other cities. However, Kish retook power several times.

Pictographs from Kish, circa 3500 BCE, that later evolved into cuneiform writing[a]

Sargon's life story picks back up in the badly damaged *Sargon and Ur-Zababa Tablet*.[ii] Despite its storied history, Kish fell into ruins until a new king, Ur-Zababa, came on the scene. He rebuilt the irrigation canals and got the pottery and metalworking factories up and running again. During Ur-Zababa's reign, Sargon grew up in Kish as the adopted son of the palace gardener. No one knows what Sargon's real name was. The name Sargon (*Sarru-kin* in Akkadian) was a title meaning "true king."

One night, Sargon brought garden produce to the palace kitchen. King Ur-Zababa was asleep and having an unsettling dream triggered by the high gods Enlil and An. Something in the dream compelled Ur-Zababa to appoint Sargon as his cupbearer when he awakened. A

---

[i] *Sumerian King List*, trans. Jean-Vincent Scheil, Stephen Langdon, and Thorkild Jacobsen (Livius, updated 2020), https://www.livius.org/sources/content/anet/266-the-sumerian-king-list/#Translation.

[ii] *Sargon and Ur-Zababa*, The Electronic Text Corpus of Sumerian Literature (Oxford: Faculty of Oriental Studies, University of Oxford, 2006), https://etcsl.orinst.ox.ac.uk/cgi-bin/etcsl.cgi?text=t.2.1.4#.

cupbearer's job was to pour the king's wine and taste it to check for poison. Because they were always nearby, cupbearers tended to be informal advisors to the kings. Becoming the king's cupbearer was a considerable step up for the humble palace gardener.

After about a week, King Ur-Zababa received news so terrifying that he wet himself. Most likely, he heard that Lugal-Zage-Si, king of Uruk, was on his way to attack Kish. Lugal-Zage-Si was a cruel conqueror who had already swept southern Sumer into his mini-empire. Now, Kish was his next target.

That night, Sargon groaned in his sleep, and the palace servants told the king they believed Sargon had had a vision. Ur-Zababa called Sargon to him.

"Tell me about your dream!" he urged.

Sargon paled but reluctantly told him, "Sire, I had a vision of the goddess Inanna. She...well...she was drowning you in a river of blood."

Ur-Zababa dismissed Sargon but chewed his lips in horror. "The dream is a prophecy! Inanna has made Sargon her favorite. She wants him to be king, which means he will kill me. I'll have to strike first!"

Thus, as our introduction story detailed, the king plotted to transform Sargon into a bronze statue. Carrying out his plan, he sent Sargon on an errand to Beliš-Tikal, the metalworker.

However, Inanna intervened. "Don't go inside the house!" she told Sargon.

Inanna (Ishtar) was a chief Mesopotamian goddess. '

Sargon met the metalworker at his front gate and survived the murder plot. King Ur-Zababa turned white when Sargon cheerfully walked back into the palace. Now, the king had to find another way to eliminate his rival.

Ur-Zababa sent Sargon to King Lugal-Zage-Si to deliver peace terms. Sargon was aware that his king meant to kill him, so he decided to switch sides and offer his services to Lugal-Zage-Si. He knew Kish inside and out and could help the king with the best plan of attack. Lugal-Zage-Si conquered Kish, placing Sargon as his vassal-king over the city around 2334 BCE. Thus, the child found in the river now ruled the great city of Kish.

A bronze sculpture found in Nineveh, probably Sargon the Great [5]

How Did Sargon Conquer and Unify the Sumerian City-States?

After Sargon helped him defeat Kish, Lugal-Zage-Si now controlled Sumer (today's southern Iraq). Sargon unsettled Lugal-Zage-Si when he turned his attention to northern Mesopotamia, uniting the Akkadian-speaking shepherds. The *Sargon and Ur-Zababa* tablet mentions an apparent intrigue between Sargon and Lugal-Zage-Si's wife, which no doubt added fuel to the fire. With his Akkadian army, Sargon marched on Uruk, the capital of his former ally.

Lugal-Zage-Si called up fifty kings of Sumer's city-states to march with him against Sargon. He thought Sargon would yield when he realized he faced such a formidable force. However, the great king soon received such horrifying news that he fell backward on the ground, exclaiming, "Alas! Sargon is not giving up!"

Sargon not only refused to back down but also utterly crushed the Sumerians. He flattened Uruk's walls and forced Lugal-Zage-Si to wear a yoke in shame. On the idol of Enlil, Lugal-Zage-Si's patron god, Sargon inscribed his breathtaking victory.

Of course, the Sumerians in the other cities did not throw open their gates to welcome Sargon. They were happy he got rid of the despot Lugal-Zage-Si, yet they wanted to return to their independent city-state system. Sargon had to march around Sumer, conquering each city in turn. It was a watershed moment when he finally held all of ancient Iraq. The Akkadian people had now replaced the Sumerians as rulers of Mesopotamia. Semitic-speaking people—the Akkadians, Assyrians, and Babylonians—governed ancient Iraq for most of the next 1,800 years until Cyrus the Great invaded from Persia (Iran).

Sargon was just getting started on his massive empire. He marched into ancient Syria, Turkey, Lebanon, and Canaan (today's Israel and Palestine), conquering as far as the Mediterranean Sea. Sargon then turned east, crossed the Zagros Mountains into Elam (Iran), and captured its capital city of Susa.

How did Sargon transform his military into such an indomitable powerhouse? He bragged of winning thirty-four wars and conquered territory stretching from the Mediterranean Sea to Iran's deserts. Before Sargon, no king had a full-time army. The fighting men were farmers, fishermen, craftsmen, and shopkeepers in the off-season. Warfare typically occurred in the summer, between the planting and harvesting of crops. Sargon had the world's first standing army of 5,400 men who could fight in any season. He could march his army five hundred miles to Syria without worrying about getting back in time for harvest.

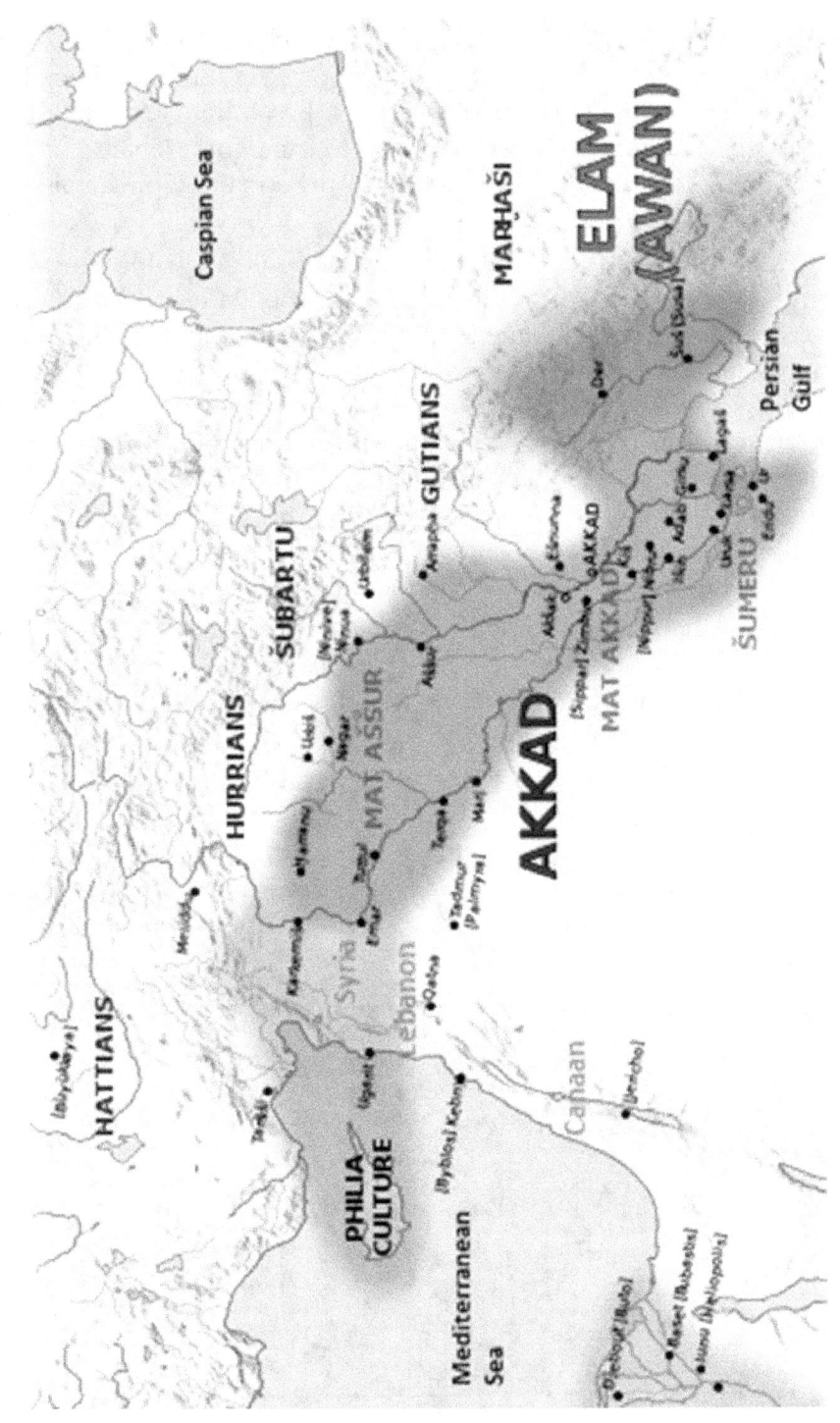

Sargon the Great's Empire [6]

Sargon also had a team of bureaucrats in charge of logistics. They arranged for siege engines to be in the right place at the right time. They ensured the troops had plenty of beer and bread and that the chariot horses and pack animals had water and feed. Cuneiform tablets that have survived to the present day document all the organization involved in maintaining Sargon's war machine.

Carvings show that the Akkadian army used spears, battle axes, bows and arrows, maces, throwing clubs, and slingshots. While the Sumerians used basic bows, the Akkadians were among the first in the world to use the composite bow with bronze arrowheads, revolutionizing warfare. The simple bows used by the Sumerians were a single piece of wood. The composite bows had layers of wood, with animal sinew and horn all glued together. Arrows shot from a composite bow flew two to three times faster and farther than arrows from a simple bow, making them far more lethal. Since they were lighter than regular bows, composite bows could be shot from horseback or chariots.

The cities that Sargon and his successors attacked had high, thick defensive walls surrounding them. As illustrated on an ancient cylinder seal, the Akkadian army had multiple ways to attack these cities.

What was a cylinder seal? The ancient Mesopotamians used these cylinders to sign their names. They were about four inches long with engraved pictures and cuneiform writing. The owner rolled the seal in a piece of damp clay, leaving the imprint of the image and words. The clay hardened to form a small disk. Tens of thousands of these cylinder seals or the disks with their imprints have survived, opening a window into Mesopotamia's ancient culture.

A battle scene from an Akkadian cylinder seal[7]

A seal from an Akkadian city depicts the tower of a city wall with soldiers at the top. Two chariots at the top right and left attack the city. At the bottom left, two soldiers push what looks like a battering ram toward the tower. Two other soldiers use the battering ram as a ramp to run up to the top of the tower. Meanwhile, at the bottom right of the scene, a soldier is pushing a tower-like contraption on wheels with a soldier inside it toward the city tower. This was probably used to protect soldiers while they shot at the city and may also have been a way to climb into the city tower.

What Administrative Systems Did Sargon Use in His Expansive Empire?

Sargon's sweeping empire encompassed multiple nations and ethnicities. He centralized the government, requiring all the lands to pay taxes. The Akkadians maintained meticulous records inscribed on clay tablets. The surviving tablets reveal their marriage arrangements, business deals, taxes, property sales, family archives, and history.

Each region kept its religion and other cultural traditions, but Akkadian was the empire's official language. Although Sumerian and Akkadian belong to different language families, they significantly influenced one another due to continuous interaction. By the end of the Akkadian Empire, Sumerian was mainly used only in temple worship, and Akkadian became the lingua franca.

What Challenges Did Sargon and His Successors Face?

It is one thing to conquer an empire and another to hold it together. The *Legend of Sargon* tells of an uprising in central and northern Mesopotamia:

> In my old age of fifty-five, all the lands revolted against me, and they besieged me in Agade, but the old lion still had teeth and claws. I went forth to battle and defeated them: I knocked them over and destroyed their vast army.[i]

Although Sargon thought he was old at fifty-five, he lived about twenty more years. Six Sumerian city-states rebelled within days after his son

---

[i] *The Legend of Sargon of Akkadê, c. 2300 BCE* (Fordham University, Internet Ancient History Sourcebook, 1999). https://sourcebooks.fordham.edu/ancient/2300sargon1.asp.

Rimush took the throne. Sargon had trounced them all five decades earlier, and they dared not rechallenge him. Yet, they may have guessed that Rimush lacked the teeth and claws his father had. It was a deadly misjudgment.

Rimush's revenge was swift and brutal. In his inscriptions, he boasted that he flattened cities, even digging their foundations out of the ground. He massacred 110,000 men in the six cities, sent 29,000 to cut stone in Elam's quarries, and exiled 25,000 Sumerians. He did not destroy two of the now-empty rebel cities—Umma and Lagash. Instead, he handed them over to his Akkadian supporters.

Naram-Sin, grandson of Sargon*

Rimush's own officials ambushed and murdered him, making his brother Manishtushu the next king for fifteen years. His son Naram-Sin became the Akkadian Empire's fourth king. Almost immediately, Naram-Sin had to confront the revolt of eighteen Sumerian cities. He defeated them so brilliantly that the citizens of Agade, the empire's capital, asked him to be their city's patron god, equal to Inanna and the other deities. Naram-Sin allowed them to build a temple to him, calling himself "the mighty god of Agade," which brought down heaven's wrath.

His downfall—and the empire's—had begun. The rains stopped. Plagues and famine struck. Gutian tribes from the east invaded and stole livestock. Farmers abandoned their fields and orchards. Without irrigation, the crops and fruit trees died, and the desert reclaimed Agade. The once-mighty empire crumbled, leaving barely a trace.

What Legacy Did the Akkadian Empire Leave Behind?

Sargon and his successors built a road network snaking out from the Euphrates and Tigris rivers. These roads reached every point of the empire. The Akkadians developed the world's first postal system and even used envelopes, although their "letters" were clay tablets. They applied a thin layer of clay over the tablet to provide privacy, which was chipped off when it reached its destination. A common language—Akkadian—unified much of the Middle East. As previously mentioned, Sargon also formed the world's first full-time military. Ultimately, the Akkadian Empire set the framework for the following Babylonian and Assyrian empires.

Chapter 2: The Great Wall and the Qin Dynasty

"He's dead! The emperor is dead!" the chief eunuch, Zhao Gao, whispered to Li Si, the prime minister.

"What? He was in perfect health yesterday!"

"He died during the night." The eunuch wrung his hands. "I...think it might have been what he drank last night. He was certain it would give him immortality."

"You mean that cursed mercury?" Li Si paced back and forth. "You're probably right. He always kept his sword in his lap for fear of assassins. Now, he has accidentally killed himself!"

"What do we do? We're in the middle of nowhere!" asked Zhao Gao, worriedly.

Li Si frowned. "We must keep his death a secret until we return to the palace. Otherwise, they'll put Fusu on the throne before we get there. You and I both know that Fusu is *not* the right person!"

"Well, he's the oldest son...but...are you thinking Ying Huhai?" Zhao Gao asked.

"Exactly! He's young and has no strength of character. You and I will run the empire!"

Zhao Gao smiled. Then his brow furled. "But the emperor...his body will start stinking! It will take weeks to get back to Xianyang."

"Fish! *Chòu yú*—stinky fish! You know how he loved the stuff. We'll fill two wagons in front of and behind his carriage. Everyone will think the foul smell is the fish."

Qin Shi Huang, the first Qin emperor [o]

Thus, China's first emperor came to an ignominious end. But how did his reign begin? How did Qin Shi Huang unify the warring states, implement sweeping reforms, and initiate grand architectural projects that left an indelible mark on China's history? What part did ambition and complex palace intrigue play in China's first, albeit brief, imperial dynasty? Let's explore the answers to these questions through the pages of ancient texts.

The *Shiji* is an ancient comprehensive history of China stretching back to the mythical Yellow Emperor (2697 BCE).[i] The author, Sima Qian, compiled it using older documents and finished it in the early first century BCE.

---

[i] Sima Qian, *Shiji, Records of the Grand Scribe*, China Knowledge: An Encyclopaedia on Chinese History and Literature, accessed March 13, 2025, http://www.chinaknowledge.de/Literature/Historiography/shiji.html.

The *Shiji* and other Chinese histories tell of the Warring States period (475-221 BCE) that spelled the end of the Zhou dynasty (1046-256 BCE), China's longest dynasty. As the Zhou dynasty grew weaker, China's states declared independence, and the seven most powerful states absorbed the smaller ones. Hundreds of wars raged between the seven states in the Warring States era as each attempted to snatch dominance.

Meanwhile, the northern and western states fought the Xiongnu, nomadic horseback-riding tribes who roamed the steppes of today's Mongolia and southeastern Russia. The Xiongnu became such a threat that the Chinese began building miles of walls about thirteen feet high to keep them out.

What Were the Legalist Principles Underpinning the Qin Administration?

In the Warring States period, the highly organized Qin state followed the philosophy of Legalism. It taught that most people let self-interest lead them astray. People are more likely to be corrupt than ethical. Thus, a government must have strict, harshly enforced laws while rewarding those with integrity.

A prominent Qin statesman, Shang Yang (390-338 BCE), promoted Legalism. He believed everyone, regardless of status, should follow the same standard of behavior and be equal before the law. Shang Yang's land reforms upended the ancient aristocratic landowner system and introduced private land ownership.

His Legalist views transformed warfare in China. Before Shang Yang, war followed strict codes of honor. An army on one side waited politely while the other side set up its positions. Winners treated the losers with honor. Most warriors were noblemen. Shang Yang dramatically increased the Qin army by requiring all men to fight and rewarding those who killed the most enemy soldiers. He ranked soldiers based on their brilliance in battle, not their social status, as in earlier days. Noblemen who refused to go to war lost their grand estates, which were divided up and given to the soldiers who proved themselves. War suddenly became much more lethal and far less polite.

Shang Yang's ideology flew in the face of the suppressed Confucian and Daoist ideologies. Shang Yang punished wrongdoers, whereas Confucianism focused on cultivating morality through patient instruction and social rituals. Confucianism taught respect for the social hierarchy, while Legalism dismantled it. Meanwhile, Daoism taught that harmony grew out of inaction and not getting too involved in the world's affairs. Yet, the ever-pragmatic Shang Yang promoted competition and striving to be the best.

Shang Yang's execution [10]

Shang Yang made enemies, especially among the ruling upper class, who were losing their land. When King Huiwen became the ruler of Qin in 338 BCE, he carried a grudge because Shang Yang had once punished him for a minor crime. Royals were seldom penalized for anything. King Huiwen got his revenge by executing Shang Yang's immediate family. He then killed Shang Yang by attaching ropes tied to his head, arms, and legs to oxcarts and pulling him to pieces. Nevertheless, Shang Yang's philosophy and reforms persevered. He had transformed the Qin military into an indomitable war machine, which led the Qin state to astounding victory.

How Did Ying Zheng Become King at Age Thirteen?

The *Shiji* says that Ying Zheng's father was ostensibly Prince Yiren, who later became King Zhuangxiang of Qin. His mother, Zhao Ji, had been a dancing girl and concubine (sexual partner) of a wealthy merchant named Lu Buwei. When Prince Yiren met Zhao Li, her beauty and charm captivated him. He asked and received permission from Lu Buwei to marry Zhao Ji. However, the whispers began when Zhao Li gave birth to a son in 259 BCE: "She was pregnant when she got married. Lu Buwei is the true father!"

The whispers grew louder when Lu Buwei manipulated events so that Prince Yiren and later Ying Zheng became king. Prince Yiren's grandfather, Zhaoxiang, was the king of Qin (306-251 BCE). Yiren's father, Xiaowen, was the crown prince. However, Yiren's mother, Lady Xia, was only a concubine, which typically meant that Yiren would not be the next king. However, Xiaowen's queen, Lady Huayang, had no children. Lu Buwei convinced Lady Huayang to adopt Yiren, which put him in the line of succession. About a year later, Yiren's grandfather died. Zhaoxiang's death brought Yiren's father, Xiaowen, to the throne, but he died three days later. Yiren became king after his father's suspiciously sudden death.

Yiren, now King Zhuangxiang (250-247 BCE), made Zhao Ji his queen, placing Ying Zheng next in line as king. He also made his wife's former lover, Lu Buwei, his prime minister. Zhuangxiang only ruled for three years before he died. Ying Zheng was only twelve or thirteen at the time, not old enough to rule independently. Lu Wei, the prime minister (and possibly Ying Zheng's father), was his regent for nine years.

China's states before its first empire [11]

How Did Ying Zheng Unify China?

Although only a young teen, Ying Zheng envisioned a unified China. His grandfather, King Zhaoxiang, had annexed the Chu and Zhao states on Qin's southeastern and northeastern borders. When Yeng Zheng was in his twenties and no longer under a regent, he began his campaign to bring all of China under Qin dominance. He revived Shang Yang's military reforms, such as incentivizing valor and rewarding soldiers who fought well.

In 230 and 228 BCE, he captured the small yet formidable Han and Wei states. The last states to fall in 221 BCE were the Qi and Yan in the northeast. The Qin now ruled all of China's major states. China's former rulers had called themselves "Wang," meaning "king." However, Ying Zheng took the title "Shi Huangdi," meaning "First Emperor."

While conquering all of China, Ying Zheng survived two assassination plots. When he marched on Yan, its crown prince, Dan, sent two assassins posing as diplomats to Ying Zheng's lodgings. They carried the severed head of Fan Yuqi, a former Qin general who had betrayed Ying

Zheng. They also had a map of Dukang, a fertile region in Yan that Ying Zheng was determined to capture. The younger assassin, Qin Wuyang, was only twelve or thirteen. He lost his nerve, sweating and shivering, and could not go near the king.

As Ying Zheng unrolled the map, the assassin Jing Ke lunged at him with his poisoned knife. King Zheng pulled away, although the blade sliced through his sleeve. He ran from the assassin, trying to pull his long sword from his belt. As Jing Ke chased him around a pillar, the royal physician, Xia Wuji, happened to walk in. He flung his medicine bag at the assassin, giving King Zheng time to pull out his sword. The king stabbed the assassin nine times, killing him, then slumped on his throne, catatonic, with his sword lying across his legs. From that moment on, he always kept his sword unsheathed on his lap.

Shortly after, Jing Ke's close friend, Gao Jianli, plotted to kill King Zheng in revenge. He was a famous player of the zhu, a Chinese stringed instrument. He appeared at Ying Zheng's camp, offering to play his instrument for the king's amusement. However, one of Zheng's attendants recognized him. Instead of killing him, King Zheng gouged Gao Jianli's eyes out so he could still play the zhu for him. He permitted the musician to sit close to him while playing. Suddenly, Gao Jianli grabbed his instrument and swung it at Zheng's head, but he missed since he was blind. Zheng had to execute him, after all.

Terracotta warrior unearthed near Qin Shi Huang's tomb [13]

What Reforms Did Qin Shi Huang Bring to China?

Qin Shi Huang reorganized his administration based on the teachings of Han Fei, a teacher of Legalism like Shang Yang. Qin Shi Huang divided his vast empire into thirty-six commanderies (provinces), subdivided into districts. Previously, members of the royal family served as provincial rulers. However, Qin Shi Huang chose administrators based on competence. He also introduced the Censorate as his watchdog, investigating corruption, misconduct, subversion, and judicial procedures.

The emperor's ancestor, King Huiwen, had begun minting round bronze coins. Qin Shi Huang made these coins the standard currency for all of China, displacing regional forms of money. Qin Shi Huang also introduced standard weights and measures. He sent bronze models of the new measurements to all the provinces so they could copy them.

The earliest surviving examples of Chinese writing are "oracle-bones"—inscriptions carved into bones and turtle shells around 1250 BCE. They started as pictographs and evolved into symbolic characters. Qin Shi Huang's scholars standardized the characters, and Prime Minister Li Si sent orders mandating this script throughout China.

Qin Shi Huang also built an incredible web of roads and canals connecting China's far-flung cities. He specified the axle width for wagons and chariots to fit his roads' standardized width. Enhanced transportation improved trade and made it easier to move his armies around as needed.

How Did Qin Shi Huang Build the Great Wall?

As previously mentioned, the Chinese built sections of walls along their northern and western borders to keep out hostile nomadic tribes like the Xiongnu, the Ordos, and the Xianyun. The Chinese had built the earliest parts of the wall by at least the seventh century BCE. The *Book of Songs*, an ancient Chinese poetry collection, has a poem about King Xuan (827-782 BCE), who ordered his general to build a wall in the north to keep the Xianyun out.

The Great Wall slithers over the mountains near Beijing. [18]

Qin Shi Huang masterminded the gargantuan task of connecting the existing sections into one wall, like a dragon creeping over the mountains and valleys. He sent General Meng Tian with 300,000 soldiers to begin bridging the gaps between wall sections and shoring up the older walls. The emperor sent 500,000 more non-military men. All Chinese men had to dedicate one year to building the wall; he also sent criminals to work on the wall. Up to a million men simultaneously labored on the wall at any given time.

The laborers endured grueling weather conditions, sandstorms, and food shortages. Countless men died from backbreaking work in near-starvation conditions. Landslides in the mountains swept them away, and they faced the constant threat of attack by wild animals.

Their construction technique was to build two parallel walls using stone, brick, or wood, depending on local resources. They filled the gap between the walls with packed earth and built beacon towers and forts at intervals. Building, rebuilding, mending, and improving the wall continued for two millennia. The Great Wall protected China and showcased a monumental human effort.

How Did Qin Shi Huang's Obsession with Immortality Play Out?

Immortality dominated the first emperor's thoughts and plans. He wanted to live forever in his mortal body if he could find a way. Otherwise, he wanted to ensure he had a happy afterlife. Chinese philosophy was vague about what happened after a person died. Legalism focused on the here and now. Confucius had little to say about life after death other than encouraging ancestor worship. Yet, for Confucius, ancestor worship was mainly about respect for their legacy. Daoism taught that when a person died, their spirit was reabsorbed into the Tao, the unknowable source of all things.

Chinese mythology told of a white spirit mountain called Mount Penglai in the middle of the sea. Eight immortal people lived in a gold and silver palace on the mountain. Fruit growing on the island's trees could cure any disease, keep a person young forever, and bring the dead back to life. The emperor sent his court sorcerer, Xu Fu, over the eastern sea in ten beautiful ships with five hundred boys and girls, commanding them, "Find the mountain and return with the magical fruit!"

An ancient painting of one of the ships in search of Mount Penglai [14]

Sorcerer Xu Fu found Japan and thought Mount Fuji was Penglai. However, unable to find the immortals or the fruit, he returned home. He set off on a second quest and never returned. When the first emperor realized Xu Fu was not coming back, he withdrew into seclusion, constantly searching for a magical herb or potion to give him immortality. As our earlier story indicates, he may have died from consuming mercury or a toxic herb.

Qin Shi Huang's "plan B" was a happy existence in the next life. He pursued both plans simultaneously. Soon after ascending the throne, he ordered over a half million laborers to build his tomb and make an army of terracotta warriors to guard it. The life-size clay figurines even included horses and his favorite pets. His tomb remains untouched to this day, as ancient inscriptions hinted at poison and booby traps that would harm any tomb robbers.

However, in 1974 CE, farmers unearthed one of the clay warriors. Since then, archaeologists have found vaults with over eight thousand terracotta soldiers, horses, bronze chariots, and weapons. The warriors have distinct facial features, suggesting they were modeled after real people.

Terracotta soldiers from a pit near Qin Shi Huang's tomb [15]

What Happened to the Dynasty after Qin Shi Huang Died?

As the story relates, after the first emperor died suddenly in 210 BCE, his prime minister, Li Si, and chief eunuch, Zhao Gao, schemed to bring a younger son, Ying Hu Hai, to the throne. Zhao Gao had tutored him from infancy and held significant sway over the teenager. Hu Hai took the throne name Qin Er Shi ("Number Two" Qin), but Zhao Gao and Li Si were the shadow government.

Lacking a strong leader at the helm, the Qin dynasty plunged into a tailspin. Widespread rebellion arose, spurred by harsh laws, heavy taxation, and forced labor. In the chaos of civil war, the empire lost 300,000 soldiers in the Battle of Ju Lu. It desperately needed more men. Li Si asked the young emperor to divert the enormous sum he was spending on building a new palace toward hiring a new army. In a fit of rage, the emperor ordered Li Si's execution.

Zhao Gao held on to power but knew he would be the erratic emperor's next target. When Qin Er Shi came to the bitter realization that he really did need more soldiers, he tried to blame Zhao Gao. However, the chief eunuch was one step ahead of him. He surrounded the emperor with his loyal men.

"Why didn't you tell me we were out of men? You should die like Li Si!" Qin Er Shi screamed.

"You killed Li Si because he *did* tell you the truth!" Zhao Gao retorted. "You are the only one to blame. You must accept responsibility and commit suicide. It is the only honorable thing to do."

Thus, after only three years on the throne, the twenty-two-year-old emperor ended his life. Zhao Gao appointed another young family member, Ying Ziying, as king, *not* emperor, as the empire had crumbled. However, on his coronation day, Ying Ziying turned on Zhao Gao and killed him. Ziying's reign was short, lasting only forty-six days before surrendering to Liu Bang, a rebel leader. Liu Bang became the emperor of the new Han dynasty, which replaced the Qin dynasty in 202 BCE.

Chapter 3: The End of the Roman Republic

Blood pooled under Lucretia from the knife she had just plunged into her chest. Her husband and father both screamed in horror, but Brutus pulled the knife from her body and held it in the air.

"By this blood, I swear, I will pursue Lucius Tarquinius Superbus and his wicked wife and children. I will not let them, nor any other, be king of Rome!"[i]

The other men raised their swords, swearing to erase Rome of its kings. They carried Lucretia's body to the Forum as an outraged crowd gathered. When they heard the king's son had violated Lucretia, they vowed to avenge her. King Tarquin fled Rome as the Romans decided to go in a new direction politically.

Thus, the Roman Republic began. Over the next five centuries, Rome morphed from an unassuming city-state into a vast realm on three continents. Yet, how did it end? What led to the Roman Republic's collapse and the Roman Empire's rise? How did social unrest and class tensions destabilize the longstanding republic? What unbridled ambition led to the political intrigues that culminated in imperial rule under Augustus? Let's explore the answers in the chapter on the Roman Republic.

---

[i] Livy, *The Rise of Rome: Books One to Five* Volume I (Oxford University Press, 2009).

How Did the Roman Republic Govern?

In 509 BCE, the idea of a republic was new. Most city-states had kings or the occasional queen. Greece's city-states had kings, tyrants (absolute rulers who seize power unconventionally), and oligarchies (rule by an unelected group). Athens was experimenting with a democracy in which all male citizens could vote.

Consul Appius Claudius Caecus enters the Senate in Roman Republic [16]

At the Roman Republic's inception, the elite patrician class ruled the working-class people called plebeians. The Republic changed with the times to deal with crises like the plebeians demanding a say in government. Rome also had to figure out how to govern all the lands it was conquering. The Republic introduced novel political concepts like checks and balances, elections, impeachments, separation of powers, term limits, and vetoes.

In the Roman Republic, two elected men, called consuls, ruled Rome together for a one-year term. Since the Republic kept busy conquering other lands, one consul typically led the army while the other handled administrative affairs. The military Centuriate Assembly elected the consuls. (In the Roman army, a century was one hundred soldiers, and each century got a vote.)

The consuls appointed the senators in the early days of the Republic. The senators advised the consuls and voted on bills. They controlled the Republic's finances, foreign policy, and day-to-day administration. If Rome had a crisis, the Senate could appoint a temporary dictator with emergency powers for a maximum of six months.

Later, the Republic added an Assembly of Tribes, representing geographic areas. This assembly could elect some officials, make laws, and judge some crimes. The working class finally got a voice in government in 494 BCE when the Republic formed the *Concilium Plebis*, or Council of the Plebs, which could propose or veto laws.

How Did Rome Expand during the Republic?

At the beginning of the Republic, Rome was a modest city-state covering about three hundred square miles, with a population of around 83,000 people. At the end of the Republic, the city of Rome had about a half million people. An estimated ten million people lived in its provinces on three continents.

During Rome's first 250 years as a monarchy, it quickly took control of central Italy. Meanwhile, Greece was establishing colonies in southern Italy. After forming its Republic, Rome began conquering the local tribes and the Greek colonies in southern Italy. By 264 BCE, Rome controlled the entire Italian peninsula. It then focused on Sicily, the large island at the toe of Italy's boot.

Up to this point, Rome had no navy. Most cities in Sicily were colonies of Greece or North Africa's Carthage, which had the world's strongest navy. From 264–146 BCE, Rome fought three Punic Wars against Carthage to take control of the Mediterranean. "Punic" comes from the word *Punicus*, Latin for the Phoenicians, a people from Lebanon who settled Carthage.

Always up for a challenge, in 261 BCE, the Romans built 120 warships for their brand-new navy. They knew the Carthaginians and Greeks had superior maneuvering skills, so they built long gangplanks to board enemy ships and fight one-to-one, which was the Roman military's superpower. They also made catapults to fling fiery projectiles at their adversaries. The Mediterranean world gasped when Rome beat Carthage in its first two sea battles. Rome even won the world's largest sea battle of all time, the Battle of Cape Ecnomus, in 256 BCE, involving 680 ships.

An ancient Roman trireme warship [17]

However, Rome suffered humiliating losses in the next few years. Two killer storms sunk 470 Roman ships. And then, in 249 BCE, Consul Appius Claudius Pulcher's sacred chickens, which he used to foretell the future, gave him news he did not like. He tossed them off the ship, cackling and squawking. When Pulcher lost the battle against Carthage, Rome stripped him of his position and charged him with sacrilege for killing the chickens.

In 218 BCE, the brilliant General Hannibal of Carthage scaled the 13,000-foot Isère Alps with his elephants and horses, invading Italy from the north. Rome barely survived Hannibal's surprise invasion but finally obliterated Carthage in 149 BCE.

Rome had been warring against the Greek city-states and colonies while simultaneously fighting Carthage. With Carthage razed to the ground, it was time to crush Greece. In 146 BCE, Rome burned Corinth to ashes, completing its conquest of the entire Greek subcontinent.

What Was the First Triumvirate?

Gnaeus Pompeius (Pompey) Magnus was a ruthless Roman general who served as consul three times. He won fame by scoring military wins in North Africa and Spain. He rounded up eight hundred pirates wreaking havoc in the eastern Mediterranean and rehabilitated them as farmers. Pompey conquered his way through Anatolia (Turkey), Syria, and Judea, consolidating Roman rule in the Middle East.

Despite capturing nine hundred cities, his loyal soldiers had little reward for years of service. Pompey wanted his men to receive farmland in the territory they had conquered so they could settle down and raise families. However, the senators in Rome were ignoring his request for land grants.

"And that's not all, Caesar!" he complained to his friend. "After all that time I spent settling affairs in the Middle East, the Senate has yet to ratify the treaties I made. Those Syrians are already stirring up trouble!"

Julius Caesar was a rising star in Roman politics who had just returned to Rome after a stunning victory in Spain. He nodded. "I feel the same way about my own troops. Our senators are only enriching themselves from our victories. Unless we transform the government, they will never pass that land allotment bill."

"Transform the government?" Pompey frowned.

"A triumvirate," Caesar explained. "You wield your influence to get me elected as consul. Everyone loves and respects you. As consul, I'll get that land bill passed for your soldiers and mine."

Pompey smiled, yet raised his eyebrows. "Who's the third person in this triumvirate?"

"Well, you and I have no money. We need someone rich enough to persuade the senators. We need the richest man in Rome," said Caesar.

"Meaning that deplorable, Crassus!" Pompey scowled. "I suppose I can endure him if it means getting farms for my men. I'm in, on one condition."

"Which is?" inquired Caesar.

"The hand of your daughter in marriage. I think I've fallen in love."

"Pompey! You're thirty years older than Julia!" came Caesar's incredulous response.

"I know, but she will have the most devoted husband in the Republic!"

Caesar laughed. "All right! It's a deal!"

The First Triumvirate: Pompey, Crassus, and Caesar [18]

After the First Triumvirate formed in 60 BCE, Pompey used his strategic friendships, and Crassus used his money to get Caesar elected. However, when Caesar tried to pass the land bill, the other consul, Bibulus, said he would veto it. An angry mob surrounded Bibulus and poured a bucket of feces over him. Bibulus slunk home and stayed there for the rest of the year, leaving Caesar in charge. Pompey threatened to unleash his soldiers on anyone trying to block the bill. It passed, along with Caesar's other bills for the working classes.

What Did Julius Caesar Accomplish in Gaul?

After his one year as consul, the Senate appointed Caesar as the proconsul (governor) of Gaul (northern Italy and southern France). He launched a campaign to subdue the Gallic (Celtic) tribes, expanding Rome's territory to include all of today's Belgium and France. He brutally massacred the Germanic Tencteri and Usipetes tribes that were migrating to Gaul. Caesar also sailed to Britain in 55 and 54 BCE, exploring the coast and marching inland as far as present-day London.

Caesar kept a running account of his exploits in his book *Bellum Gallicum* (*Gallic Wars*). At the end of each year, he sent a section of his book back to Rome with lively tales of his daring conquests. Although probably embellished, the stories enhanced Caesar's popularity.

How Did the First Triumvirate End?

The First Triumvirate crumbled while Caesar was in Gaul. In 52 BCE, Pompey's wife (Caesar's daughter, Julia) died in childbirth. The strain of grief and a growing rivalry between the two men dissolved their friendship. The following year, Crassus was decapitated in the Battle of Carrhae in Anatolia.

Caesar was now a renowned war hero with a seasoned army. Meanwhile, Roman politics had fallen into scandalous disarray. Politicians publicly accepted bribes. Senators fought for their bills with swords, staining the Senate floor with blood. The chaos in Rome made it increasingly apparent that the Republic was no longer functioning.

People whispered, "Perhaps we should return to a single, strong leader, like what Rome had in its earliest days."

The Romans who were entertaining ideas of a monarchy favored Pompey. Yet, Caesar wanted that ultimate power.

Roman Republic, 50 BCE [19]

How Did Caesar Trigger a Civil War?

Caesar finished his tour of duty in Gaul and marched back to Rome in 49 BCE. The Senate demanded that he disband his legions before entering Rome. Yet, Caesar crossed the Rubicon River into central Italy with five thousand men. He knew the Senate was planning to prosecute him for legal irregularities when he had been consul. He had reached the point of no return. It was either endure punishment from the Senate or take control of Rome.

Who Won the War?

As Caesar closed in on Rome, most senators fled to southern Italy. Caesar helped himself to the state treasury but harmed no one. His priority was eliminating Pompey, who had sailed to Greece yet left most of his legions in Spain. Caesar marched to Spain with less than one thousand men, defeated Pompey's army, and returned to Rome.

After having himself declared a temporary dictator, Caesar presided over the elections that made him the new consul. Now, it was time to sail to Greece and confront Pompey. Caesar put his relative, Mark Antony, in charge of Italy in his absence. In 48 BCE, Caesar and Pompey faced off in the Battle of Pharsalus in the Thessaly region of Greece. It was an epic win for Caesar. He reported that he lost only two hundred men while killing sixty thousand of Pompey's soldiers.

Pompey escaped to Egypt, a fatal mistake. Egypt had two pharaohs: thirteen-year-old Ptolemy XIII and his older sister and wife, Cleopatra VII. The siblings were at war, each wanting total control. Ptolemy XIII killed Pompey, knowing he was on the run from Caesar. Ptolemy guessed that Caesar would ultimately rule Rome and wanted to be on the right side of history.

When Caesar arrived shortly after, Ptolemy handed him Pompey's head, hoping Caesar would help him fight Cleopatra. Yet, Caesar was appalled at his one-time friend's shameful death. He mourned Pompey and organized a state funeral. Cleopatra arrived soon after and won over Caesar with her sexual wiles. The two lovers fought against Ptolemy XIII, who drowned while escaping their armies.

What Happened When Caesar Became "Dictator for Life"?

Caesar's only biological son, Caesarion, was born to Cleopatra in 47 BCE. Caesar returned to Rome and installed Cleopatra and her baby in his country villa. He ruled Rome for the next three years as consul or dictator. Caesar introduced reforms to relieve debt for the working class and help with unemployment. He was popular with ordinary people but hated by the aristocratic politicians. Caesar devised the "Julian calendar" with 365 days and a leap year every four years, adding a day in February. We use this calendar today with slight modifications.

Cleopatra VII and her son Caesarion on a mural in Pompeii[20]

Rome's dictators were not supposed to serve more than six months, yet Caesar became "dictator for life" in February 44 BCE. He was essentially a king, although he refused to wear a crown. Around sixty senators plotted to kill Caesar and restore the Republic. They murdered him on March 15 (the Ides of March), 44 BCE, in the Senate, stabbing him twenty-three times. However, his funeral ended in an uproar by the plebeians, who chased the senators out of Italy.

What Was the Aftermath of Caesar's Assassination?

Although Caesar named his nephew and adopted son Octavian as his heir, Mark Antony, Rome's new consul, tried to block Octavian's inheritance. Rome staggered on the brink of civil war with the plebeians supporting Octavian against Mark Antony. After his one year as consul ended, Antony was appointed as Macedonia's governor by the Senate. However, he wanted to be governor of northern Italy (Cisalpine Gaul) instead and marched there with his army. The Senate sent Octavian to bring him back. Before Octavian got to northern Italy, Antony crossed the Alps into France (Transalpine Gaul) and launched a conspiracy with its governor, Lepidus.

How Did the Second Triumvirate Form?

Octavian returned to Rome to discover that the underhanded senators were planning to kill him and had already appointed Brutus, one of Caesar's murderers, as the army's commander. Yet, about half of the military had fought under Caesar and transferred their ardent loyalty to his adoptive son, Octavian. With military support, Octavian announced he was Rome's consul. Yet, he needed an alliance to confront the treacherous senators. He reached out to his former enemy, Antony, and allied with him and Lepidus. Octavian sweetened the pot by offering Antony rule over Rome's eastern provinces. Thus, the Second Triumvirate burst onto the political scene in 43 BCE.

The Second Triumvirate successfully squelched the senators, but it was short-lived. Octavian and Lepidus quarreled. Then, Antony fell under Cleopatra's spell and agreed to appoint Caesarion, her son by Caesar, as Caesar's heir. Their plan was for Antony and Cleopatra to rule Rome as Caesarion's regents. When Octavian uncovered the plot, he declared war on the lovers.

How Did Octavian's Victory End the Roman Republic?

The deciding showdown was the massive Battle of Actium in the Ionian Sea off Greece's coast in 31 BCE. Octavian's maritime commander, Agrippa, led 400 ships against the combined 480 ships of Antony and Cleopatra. King Herod of the Jews, King Malchus of Arabia, and the rulers of Libya, Cilicia, and Thrace allied with Cleopatra and Antony.

Antony commanded his captains, "Do *not* try to fight in the open sea! Agrippa's ships are faster, and they will have the advantage there. Stay in the straits." Nevertheless, some of his captains ignored his orders and sailed into the Ionian Sea, where they were easily surrounded by Octavian's ships. Fearing all was lost, Cleopatra ordered her sixty ships to abandon the battle and sail to Egypt. In dismay, Antony watched his lover and her navy disappear over the horizon. He abandoned the battle to follow her, leaving about half his ships entangled with the Roman vessels. Eventually, Octavian chased the co-conspirators down. When Antony's troops abandoned him, he fell on his sword. Cleopatra also committed suicide, and Octavian seized Egypt as a Roman province.

Octavian's long-term plan was to be emperor for life, but he pretended to support the traditional semi-democratic Republic. He introduced changes incrementally. The Senate made his secret ambition easy to achieve. When he was appointed as consul shortly after returning to Rome, the Senate gave him more authority than a consul usually had and extended his term past the one-year limit. They handed the administration of the provinces to Octavian, along with complete control of the military. Octavian conquered more of Africa, Europe, and the Middle East, doubling the Republic's size.

Octavian, who became Caesar Augustus, Rome's first emperor [21]

Octavian pretended humility, refusing to wear a kingly purple robe. Yet, in 27 BCE, the Senate gave him the title of *Augustus* (magnificent) and *Princeps Senatus/Princeps Civitatis* (first in the Senate, first over the citizens). Julius Caesar had been his adoptive father, so he took the name "Caesar" and was called "Caesar Augustus" from that point. The name "Caesar" became a title for future emperors.

In Caesar Augustus's lifetime, Rome transitioned from a republic to an empire, with one man holding power. Most Romans welcomed the transition, treasuring the peace, economic stability, and wealth Augustus brought to Rome.

Chapter 4: Cleopatra's Egypt

Cleopatra VII's Egypt was the end of an era. She and her teenage son were the last pharaohs of Egypt, the end of the Ptolemaic dynasty. Although remembered as a seductress, Cleopatra was a cunning leader, navigating complex and treacherous politics. She was a multilingual scholar, strategist, and diplomat. Her chief goal was to preserve Egypt's independence and her role as pharaoh. Hers is the story of the interplay between personal relationships and political power during a pivotal era in ancient history.

How Did the Ptolemaic Dynasty Begin?

When Alexander the Great rode into Egypt in 332 BCE, his childhood friend and trusted general Ptolemy rode by his side. The Egyptians cheered, welcoming Alexander as their savior from bitter Persian rule. They had no choice. Alexander of Macedonia had already conquered all of Greece, crossed into Asia, and marched down the Mediterranean coastline with his vast army.

Most cities had politely welcomed Alexander, but Tyre resisted, and Alexander crucified their men. Gaza resisted, and Alexander crushed their seemingly insurmountable walls. The Persian king, Darius III, had ambushed Alexander near Syria's northern border. However, Alexander's impeccably trained army swiftly moved into battle formation and put up a formidable defense. An unnerved Darius swung his chariot around and raced off, leaving his soldiers, mother, wife, and daughters behind. The Egyptians pragmatically decided to welcome the Greeks.

Alexander explored Egypt and found the northern Delta region enchanting. This is where the Nile splits into multiple branches, emptying into the Mediterranean. He excitedly made elaborate plans for a new city named Alexandria, where the westernmost branch of the Nile flowed into the sea. Alexandria would be a premier trade hub and a riveting center of art, poetry, and the sciences.

Alexander never saw Alexandria in all its glory. He left no capable heir when he died of fever at age thirty-two. His generals divided up his newly conquered empire, and General Ptolemy took Egypt. He immediately set to work fulfilling Alexander's dreams—and his own. Ptolemy finished building the gleaming city of Alexandria, the "jewel of the Mediterranean," and made it Egypt's new capital.

Ptolemy and his descendants ruled as Egypt's pharaohs for 275 years, Egypt's longest dynasty. This was Cleopatra's Egypt. Although not Egyptian, they created a fusion of Egyptian and Greek culture. The Ptolemies rebuilt Egypt's temples, desecrated by the Persians, and built temples to Greek gods in Alexandria. They introduced stunning innovations that rocked the world.

How Did the Ptolemaic Dynasty Enrich the World?

Egypt soared to unprecedented heights under its first three Ptolemaic pharaohs. Ptolemy built Alexandria's Great Library for his lofty goal of collecting every book in the world. The Library at Alexandria held 490,000 books by his grandson's reign. Ptolemy imported scholars who revolutionized math, philosophy, science, art, and literature.

Two scholars at the library were the geometry geniuses Euclid and Eratosthenes. Euclid of Alexandria wrote *The Elements*, a textbook covering number theory, mathematic proofs, and geometry, including the Pythagorean Theorem. Eratosthenes was the lead librarian, renowned for calculating the earth's circumference. On June 21 (the longest day of sunlight), he plunged a stick into the ground at noon and measured its shadow's angle. Meanwhile, his assistant did the same in Syene, south of Alexandria. They compared measurements against the distance between Alexandria and Syene. Eratosthenes calculated the Earth's circumference at 28,000 miles, astoundingly close to today's calculations of 24,901 miles.

The Library of Alexandria was the world's intellectual hub.[22]

One of Eratosthenes's students at the Library of Alexandria was the teenage Archimedes of Syracuse. After returning to Sicily, he constantly exchanged letters with Eratosthenes. Archimedes estimated square roots and pi (π)—the ratio of circumference to diameter in a circle. His estimate for pi was between 3.14585 and 3.14084. (Modern-day mathematicians estimate pi as 3.1415926535.) Archimedes also developed the compound pulley, which he used to move a ship. His fascination with moving big objects led him to introduce the "Law of the Lever," utilizing a fulcrum and stick to move a heavy weight.

The philosopher Strato was Aristotle's student who moved to Alexandria and tutored Ptolemy II. Strato thought the stars were fiery like the sun. Yet, he understood that some "stars" (planets) and the moon reflect the sun's light. One of Strato's students at Alexandria was

Aristarchus of Samos. He was the first to theorize (1,800 years before Copernicus) that the Earth and other planets traveled in orbits around the sun. He taught that the stars were faraway suns and that the Earth revolved on an axis each day.

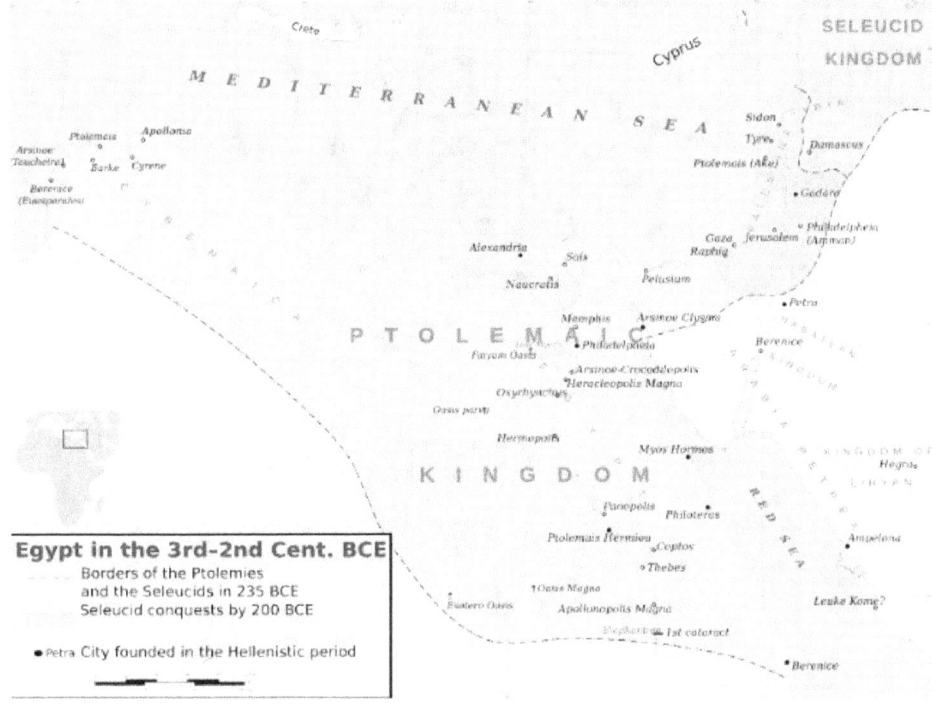

Ptolemaic Empire[88]

Ptolemy I expanded Egypt's realm to include Judea, Phoenicia, and the islands of Rhodes and Cyprus. He built the most powerful navy in the Mediterranean world. His reputation for paying the highest wages and giving land grants to veteran soldiers enabled him to hire elite sailors.

Ptolemy's son, Ptolemy II Philadelphus, became Egypt's next pharaoh in 284 BCE, leading the Ptolemaic dynasty into its golden age.

While some scholars at the library developed metaphysics and math, others dived into literature. One of the librarians, Zenodotus, was an epic poet, an editor of Homer, and a lecturer on Hesiod and Pindar. His assistants edited the Greek comedies and tragedies. Ptolemy II invited the Greek poets Callimachus, Theocritus, and Apollonius of Rhodes to teach at the Great Library's school.

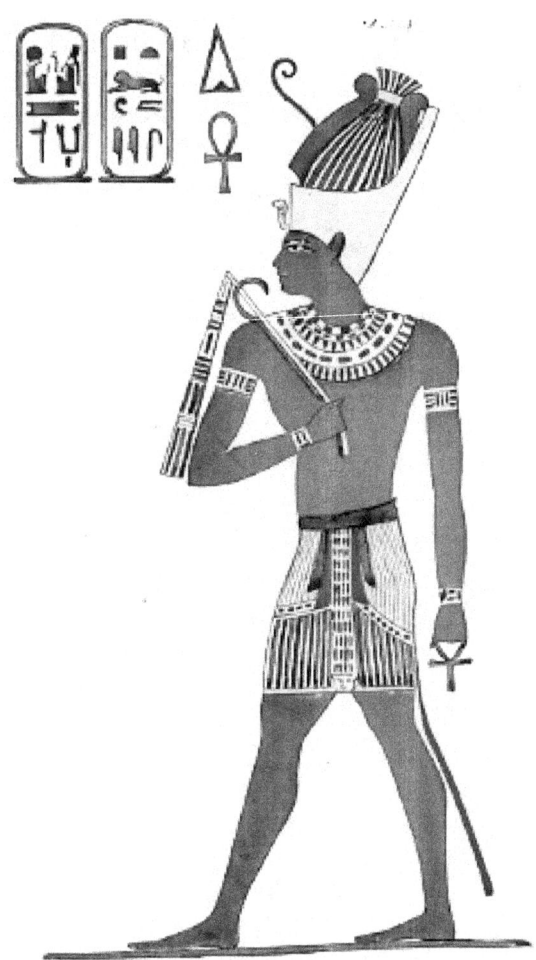

Ptolemy II Philadelphus "

Ptolemy II's oldest son, Ptolemy III Euergetes, became pharaoh in 246 BCE. Ptolemy III's sister, Berenice Syra, was married to the Seleucid Empire's king, Antiochus II Theos. When Antiochus suddenly died, probably by poison, Berenice desperately messaged her brother. She was terrified that her husband's other wife, Laodice, would kill her and her baby son. Ptolemy III marched north to Antioch in Syria but arrived too late. Laodice had murdered his sister and her baby. Ptolemy III had Laodice killed and took over Syria, Anatolia, and ancient Iraq. He retrieved treasures the Persians had stolen centuries earlier and returned them to Egypt's ancient temples.

Ptolemy III expanded Ptolemaic Egypt to its greatest extent, controlling the Mediterranean coast from Libya to today's Turkey.

What Plunged the Ptolemaic Kingdom into a Tailspin?

After Ptolemy III, the dynasty went downhill. Ptolemy IV Philopator, son of Ptolemy III, lacked interest in leadership. His friends, Agathocles and Sosibius, ran a shadow government. Southern Egypt rebelled and declared independence in 205 BCE. The following year, Ptolemy IV and his wife both died about the same time, possibly assassinated.

With Agathocles as his regent, the dead couple's little son, Ptolemy V Epiphanes, became Egypt's pharaoh at age five. In 202 BCE, Alexandria's citizens rebelled, ripped Agathocles apart, and installed a new regent.

With Egypt destabilized, Antiochus the Great of the Seleucid Empire conquered Syria. When he marched south to Judea, the Jews opened the gates of Jerusalem to him. They cheered him as their liberator from the Egyptians with no inkling of the horror to come.

At age fourteen, Ptolemy V officially became Egypt's pharaoh. The Egyptian priests inscribed the event on the Rosetta Stone in Greek, Egyptian hieroglyphics, and the Egyptian Demotic script. Two thousand years later, scholars used the Greek inscription to translate the Egyptian hieroglyphics, unlocking Egypt's ancient history.

Ptolemy V and Antiochus declared peace, yet Antiochus kept Judea, Syria, and Anatolia. Ptolemy V married Antiochus's daughter, Cleopatra Syra. Ptolemy V then warred against the southern Egypt rebels and reunited the country in 186 BCE. When he died suddenly in 180 BCE, the rumors erupted:

"He was only thirty! They must have poisoned him."

"Who? And why?"

"Antiochus the Great just died, and Ptolemy planned to recapture Judea and Syria. Yet, his advisors didn't want the war debt."

Coin of Ptolemy V Epiphanes[25]

The Ptolemaic Kingdom plunged deeper and faster into chaos. Ptolemy V's six-year-old son, Ptolemy VI Philometor, became pharaoh with Cleopatra Syra as his regent. At sixteen, Ptolemy VI married his sister, Cleopatra II. Their unhinged uncle, Antiochus IV Epiphanes, ruled the Seleucid Empire in West Asia. He attacked Egypt, taking the southern regions and capturing Ptolemy VI. The Alexandrians crowned Ptolemy VI's younger brother, Ptolemy VIII, their new pharaoh.

Antiochus Epiphanes left for Syria in 169 BCE, leaving Ptolemy VI as pharaoh in the south, while Ptolemy VIII ruled the north. Finally, their sister, Cleopatra II, devised a plan in which the three would rule together over a united Egypt. That brought Antiochus Epiphanes back to Egypt in a rage.

However, Rome inserted itself to get a foothold in Egypt. The Roman proconsul, Popillius, stopped Antiochus Epiphanes outside Alexandria. He drew a line around him in the sand. "The Roman Senate orders you to leave Egypt. Don't leave that circle until I have an answer for the Senate!" he demanded.

Antiochus had no choice but to return to Syria, taking out his wrath on Judea on the way home. He killed forty thousand Jews, placed a statue of Zeus in Jerusalem's temple, and sacrificed a pig to it. The outraged Jews started the Maccabean Revolt, won independence, and negotiated a friendly relationship with Egypt.

The following nine decades involved constant intrigue, murder, and mayhem. Two or three family members usually ruled Egypt together, but Egypt grew weaker. Meanwhile, Rome grew stronger, conquering most of the Greek world and leaving Egypt with few allies. The siblings in the royal family continued to marry each other but fought so bitterly that, by 80 BCE, they had killed each other off, leaving no legitimate heir to Egypt's throne.

How Was Cleopatra VII's Childhood Upended?

Ptolemy XII Auletes was a pharaoh's son, but his mother was only a concubine. He normally would not have become pharaoh in 80 BCE, but Egypt had no one else. Cleopatra VII, born in 69 BCE, was the second of his five children. When she was a toddler, Crassus and Julius Caesar wanted to conquer Egypt but could not convince the Senate.

When Cleopatra was six, the Roman general Pompey conquered Anatolia and Syria. Only Judea stood between Pompey and Egypt. Cleopatra's father bribed Pompey with eight thousand cavalry and a gold crown to leave Egypt in peace. Judea fell to Rome, but Egypt survived.

When Cleopatra was nine, Rome's First Triumvirate formed. Her father traveled to Rome with a bribe that equaled Egypt's annual revenue. This broke Egypt's treasury, but Julius Caesar declared Ptolemy XII as *socius et amicus* (ally and friend), and Rome formally allied with Egypt.

Yet, the following year, Rome snatched the island of Cyprus, which belonged to Egypt. This infuriated the Egyptians, and they kicked Ptolemy XII out of Egypt in 58 BCE. He fled to Rome with Cleopatra VII, now eleven years old. Her older sister, Berenice IV, became pharaoh. General Pompey took Cleopatra and her father into his home.

Ptolemy XII borrowed a fortune to bribe Aulus Gabinius, the Roman proconsul of Syria, to help him take Egypt back. In 55 BCE, Gabinius's army, led by Mark Antony, restored Cleopatra's father to Egypt's throne. Her father killed her older sister, Berenice IV, who had been trying to convince Rome to keep her on the throne and her father out of Egypt.

This was the milieu in which Cleopatra grew up. Despite the turmoil of her childhood, Cleopatra received a stellar education, with the Greek philosopher Philostratus as her tutor. Unlike most Ptolemaic pharaohs, who only communicated in Greek, Cleopatra learned to speak, read, and write in Egyptian. Having spent her early teen years in Rome, she had also learned Latin. Additionally, she knew the Syrian, Aramaic, and Ethiopian languages.

Why Did Cleopatra Become Julius Caesar's Lover?

In 51 BCE, Cleopatra's father died when she was eighteen. She married her eleven-year-old brother, Ptolemy XIII Theos Philopator, and they ruled as co-pharaohs. At least, that was their father's plan. However, Ptolemy XIII and his regent, Pothinus, plotted against Cleopatra, and a civil war raged for several years. When her brother prevailed, Cleopatra fled to Syria for reinforcements.

While Cleopatra was in Syria, Pompey arrived in Egypt, and her brother's men ambushed and killed him. When Julius Caesar got to Egypt shortly after, he was furious that Ptolemy XIII had killed Pompey. Ptolemy XIII escaped, but Caesar executed Pothinus. At this point, Cleopatra sailed back to Egypt and heard what had just happened. She decided her best scheme was to ally with Caesar against her brother.

Cleopatra charms Caesar [26]

Cleopatra wasn't a classic beauty, but she knew how to make an entrance. The Greek historian Plutarch said Cleopatra had a servant smuggle her in a sack into the palace where Caesar was staying. Caesar looked up to see her gracefully rising from the bundle in a diaphanous gown. One glance, and she captured Caesar's attention and held it until he died.

Caesar and Cleopatra won the war, and she was reinstated as Egypt's pharaoh, co-ruling with another younger brother, Ptolemy XIV. Cleopatra gave birth to Caesar's son, Caesarion, in 47 BCE. Three years later, Cleopatra was staying in Caesar's villa near Rome when the senators murdered him. She fled back to Egypt. Three months later, her brother and co-pharaoh Ptolemy XIV died. He was only fifteen, and people speculated that she poisoned him to elevate three-year-old Caesarion as her co-pharaoh.

How Did Cleopatra Seduce Mark Antony?

Before Caesar's murder, Mark Antony had been his right-hand man. Antony officiated at Caesar's funeral and assumed he would be his political heir. However, Caesar's will crushed his expectations. Caesar named Octavian as his adopted son and heir to his estate. At first, Mark Antony opposed Octavian. Yet, as the last chapter covered, he soon realized it was better to be allies than enemies, so he formed the Second Triumvirate with Octavian and Lepidus.

Octavian gave Mark Antony rule over Rome's eastern provinces, so he sailed to Tarsus on Turkey's southern coast. In 41 BCE, Mark Antony messaged Cleopatra to meet with him to renew Egypt's alliance with Rome. Cleopatra decided to make another unforgettable entrance. Flutes and lyres played as she sailed into the harbor in an exquisite boat propelled by silver oars and purple sails. Dressed as the goddess Aphrodite, she reclined in the ship, fanned by small boys dressed as cupids. Antony immediately fell under her spell. He sailed back to Egypt with Cleopatra, and in the following year, she gave birth to twins, Alexander Helios and Cleopatra Selene. Cleopatra also provided Antony with ships for his Parthian campaign against ancient Iran.

Cleopatra gave birth to another son by Antony, Ptolemy Philadelphus, in 36 BCE. Rome bristled when they heard of a celebration the couple staged in 34 BCE, called the Donations of Alexandria. Antony and Cleopatra dressed as deities and named their children as rulers of Roman provinces.

Bust of Cleopatra VII[27]

Disaster loomed for the lovers when Octavian found Antony's will in 32 BCE. Antony had left it with the Vestal Virgins at Rome's Temple of Vesta. Octavian was shocked when Antony announced that Cleopatra's son, Caesarion, was Caesar's biological son and rightful heir. That directly challenged Octavian's status as Caesar's adopted son. Octavian declared war on the couple, which ended in disaster for Antony and Cleopatra at the Battle of Actium, as we shared in the last chapter.

How Did Cleopatra's Egypt End?

Back in Egypt and full of restless energy, Cleopatra desperately tried to find a way to escape. She needed to find a place of safety with her children, but where? No viable solution emerged. Antony sat like a statue, drunk and drained of emotion. He finally roused when Octavian's ships appeared on the horizon in July 30 BCE. Antony led his troops to battle, and, at first, they were winning. Yet, his troops seemed to realize they were on the wrong side of history and deserted to Octavian.

All hope was gone. After stabbing himself, Antony bled out in Cleopatra's arms. Cleopatra knew she would be dragged to Rome and forced to march in chains at a triumph parade. That was unthinkable. When Octavian arrived, he found Cleopatra dead as well. Although legend says she died from a snake bite, none of the Roman-era historians mentioned it. A mural in Pompeii, painted several decades later, shows her wearing her crown and holding a bowl, presumably of poison. Her teenage son Caesarion, also wearing his diadem, supports her from behind.

A mural from Pompeii, probably of Cleopatra's suicide [28]

Mark Antony had requested burial in Egypt in his will, and Octavian honored that. He buried Antony and Cleopatra in the same tomb in Alexandria. Octavian killed Cleopatra's oldest son, Caesarion. As Caesar's biological son, he would complicate things for Octavian's planned future as Rome's emperor. Octavian took Cleopatra and Antony's three young children back to Rome, and his sister raised them in her home.

Cleopatra's Egypt had reached the end. It was no longer independent or ruled by the Ptolemaic dynasty. It was now *Aegyptus*, a Roman province, although Alexandria's Hellenistic culture continued to thrive.

Chapter 5: Genghis Khan and the Mongol Empire

How did a nomadic herder named Temujin rise from obscurity to unite the Mongol tribes and reshape the geopolitical landscape of Asia and Europe? What genius military and administrative strategies enabled him to impact history so powerfully? This chapter explores the legendary Genghis Khan and the Mongol Empire.

Who Were the Mongols?

The Mongol tribes herded sheep, goats, long-horned cattle, yaks, and Bactrian camels. They raced their short, pony-like horses over the steppes of Central Asia. From their humble origins in the Khentii Mountains of northern Mongolia, they eventually ruled from China to the Danube River in Eastern Europe. The Mongols blended ancestor worship, shamanism, and the worship of spirits in nature. Their primary god was Tengri, ruler of the sky and heaven. Some Mongols eventually adopted Islam or Christianity.

Temujin, later known as Genghis Khan, was born into the Mongolian Borjigin clan in 1162 CE. *The Secret History of the Mongols*, written by an unknown Mongol in Temujin's lifetime, said his ancestor, Qaidu (Kaidu), was the first to unite the Mongol people. Qaidu joined forces with the Jurchen Jin people of Manchuria in northeast China to overthrow the Liao dynasty. Qaidu also feuded fiercely against the Tayichiud, a clan formed by his wayward youngest son, Charaqai Lingqu.

Qaidu's grandson (Temujin's great-grandfather) was Khabul (Qabul) Khan. When he visited the new Jin emperor, Xi Zong, his gluttony scandalized the Chinese. Worse yet, he got roaring drunk and pulled the emperor's beard. After expelling him in disgrace, the Chinese realized they had forgotten to get his oath of loyalty to the emperor. That was the point of inviting him in the first place. "We need to bring him back!" they said.

When Khabul noticed the Chinese were following him, he suspected treachery. He and his companions ambushed and killed the Jin group, leading to brutal warfare between the Mongols and the Jin. Curiously, although Khabul had seven sons, he named a Tayichiud clan leader, Amba Ghai, as his successor. Amba Ghai captured twenty forts along the Great Wall of China, giving the Mongols the upper hand.

Mongol warriors painted by Rashid-ad-Din, a physician and advisor in the Mongol court [29]

The Jin reached out to the Tartars, another steppe tribe. The Tartars tricked Amba Ghai into thinking they wanted a marriage alliance. However, when Amba Ghai arrived with his daughter, they captured him and handed him over to the Jin, who crucified him. As he was dying, Amba Ghai screamed for his fellow Mongols to avenge his death.

The Borjigin clan reclaimed their rulership over the Mongols and elected Khabul's son, Qutula (Hotula), as their leader. However, the feud between the Borjigin and Tayichiud clans raged on. In 1161 CE, a year before Temujin was born, the Jin and Tartars attacked the Mongols, nearly annihilating the Borjigin clan and killing Qutula.

Yesugei, Temujin's father and Khabul's son, became the next Mongol leader. He had been leading a ragtag guerilla band of Mongols. Although he had a wife and concubines, a girl named Hö'elün caught Yesugei's eye. Hö'elün was already engaged to Yehe Chiledu, chief of the Merkits. Undeterred, Yesugei swept in and carried Hö'elün off, igniting a blood feud between the Merkits and the Borjigin.

What Were the Harsh Realities of Temujin's Childhood?

Temujin was born into this messy situation as Hö'elün's oldest son by Yesugei. He had two older half-brothers by his father's official wife. A typical Mongol boy, Temujin learned to ride a horse as a toddler and sped over icy lakes on skates made from bone. He learned herding, hunting, and hand-to-hand combat, but not reading and writing. His best friend was Jamukha (Jamuga). They took an *anda* oath as small boys—a solemn, spiritual vow of perpetual brotherhood and loyalty.

When Temujin was nine, his father arranged his marriage. (Mongolians got engaged as children and married in their teens. Aristocratic Mongol boys typically married high-born girls from the Ongud tribe, a Turkish people who adopted Mongol culture and lived in southeastern Mongolia. Ongud women were the beauties of the steppes.)

The bride-to-be was ten-year-old Börte, daughter of Chief Dai Sechen. However, Yesugei only had one horse for the bride price. Dai Sechen snorted and said, "I'll accept that as a down payment, but you must pay the full bride price before the wedding! Leave Temujin here with me. My son Alchi-Noyan likes him, and the boy can work to earn part of the bride price."

When Yesugei was preparing to leave, Dai Sechen approached him and said, "I had the strangest dream last night. A falcon was clutching the sun in one talon and the moon in the other. Temujin was right there. My vision must mean your boy will rule the world!"

Yesugei smiled. The future looked promising. Temujin spent the next three years as a herder for his future father-in-law. At age twelve,

Temujin received devastating news. The Tartars had invited his father to a banquet, then slipped a slow-acting poison into his food. A few hours after leaving the Tartar's camp, Yesugei suffered excruciating stomach cramps. "Monklik," he gasped to his right-hand man, "I'm dying! Go now! Get Temujin."

Monklik raced off as Yesugei died in agony. Dai Sechen scowled at the news and responded, "If I let the boy go now, what will happen to my daughter?"

Monklik reassured Dai Sechen. "They can still marry when they are older. But Temujin needs to assert himself as the new khan."

"Yes, yes. I know," grumbled Dai Sechen. "If he's not there, someone else will grab his position."

By the time Monklik retrieved Temujin and raced with him back to the steppes, it was too late. Temujin's Borjigin clansmen had decided the twelve-year-old was too young to rule. "We're taking back rulership!" the Tayichiud clan announced.

The Mongols abandoned the widow Hö'elün, taking the flocks with them. Hö'elün was left with nothing but several horses and her sons. They had to live off the land—hunting, fishing, foraging for berries, and digging roots. The sons of Yesugei's first wife harassed them, stealing the fish and game they caught.

When Temujin was thirteen, he filled the body of his older half-brother, Begter, with arrows.

Hö'elün tore into Temujin. "What were you thinking, killing your half-brother? You're like a mad dog that eats itself!"

The Tayichiud leader, Tar Gutai, decided to enslave thirteen-year-old Temujin. "He needs to be punished for killing his older brother!" he declared.

Tar Gutai put Temujin in a cangue, or "Chinese death cage," something like stocks (a large board with a hole in the middle for the person's head). One night, the guard fell asleep, and Temujin snuck off and hid in the river reeds. The next day, Sorqan Shira, a man from the Suldus tribe, found Temujin and hid him in his tent. Temujin made his escape that night and returned to his family.

When Temujin was fourteen, the Tayichiud stole eight of his family's nine horses. With the remaining horse, Temujin charged after them, tracking the raiders for four days. He met a young teen named Bo'orchu, who gave him food, water, and a fresh horse. Bo'orchu rode with Temujin for three more days until they caught up with the Tayichiud.

They snuck into the Tayichiud campsite by night, taking back the stolen horses. The Tayichiud awakened and chased after the young teens. Their chieftain rode the fastest stallion and pulled ahead of his men. As the chieftain approached, Bo'orchu twisted around in his saddle and shot an arrow into his chest. His companions stopped to tend to their chief, giving the boys time to escape.

Bo'orchu's father provided the boys with more horses and warriors. Temujin's future father-in-law, Dai Sechen, also sent reinforcements. Suddenly, Temujin segued from foraging for a living to becoming a young warlord. His experiences up to this point armed him with resilience, strategic thinking, and a relentless drive for power.

How Did Temujin Unify the Mongol Clans?

Temujin redeemed his bride when he was fifteen. Börte's mother gifted Temujin's mother with an exquisite sable coat to honor the family union. However, over a year passed, and Börte did conceive.

Meanwhile, the Merkits plotted revenge for Temujin's father stealing Hö'elün from their chief years earlier. About two years after Temujin's marriage, the Merkits kidnapped Börte.

Temujin allied with his father's friend, Toghril (Toghrul), chief of the Keraites, a powerful Turkish Mongolian tribe. He regifted the sable coat given to his mother to seal the deal. Temujin was delighted to discover his beloved childhood friend, Jamuga, had joined Toghril's band. With Toghril's substantial military force, they launched a campaign, scattering the Merkits and almost exterminating them.

Temujin got Börte back, yet he was disturbed to discover she was pregnant by a Merkit chieftain. Temujin spread the story that she was already pregnant when captured. He accepted the baby as his own and named him Jochi.

Temujin's old friend Jamuga had nearly twenty thousand troops, far more than Temujin. "He's a loose cannon!" Börte warned. Hö'elün backed her daughter-in-law's opinion.

The women were right. Jamuga picked a quarrel with Temujin, something about Temujin's sheep and Jamuga's horses. Deeply hurt, Temujin packed up his people and herds and slipped away one night, setting up a new camp.

The Mongols had to decide who they would follow. About thirteen thousand Mongols defected to Jamuga, but the rest supported Temujin, including the Borjigin clan. Temujin immediately began training his men and promoting those who proved themselves. He consistently rewarded merit over social status.

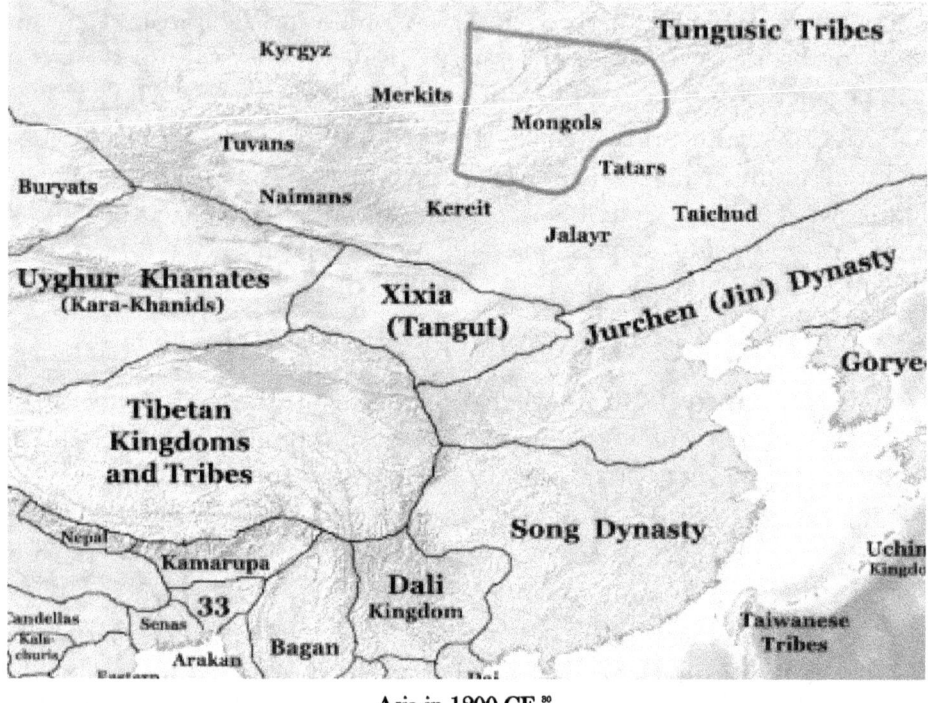

Asia in 1200 CE [80]

In 1186, after nine years of marriage, Börte gave birth to her second son and Temujin's first. He named him Ögedei. A year after that, Temujin's friend killed Jamuga's brother because he stole his horses. "This calls for war!" Jamuga screamed. With his fighting force outnumbering Temujin's three to one, Jamuga won the battle but suffered a debilitating loss of men.

How Did Temujin Become "Genghis Khan" or "Universal Ruler"?

The Chinese Jin recruited the Tartars to help them subdue the Ongud tribe, who lived close to China's northern border. The Chinese-Tartar coalition won the battle, but then the Tartars and Jin fought over the battle spoils. When the Ongud tribe heard, they swept in and utterly defeated the Jin in 1196 CE.

Ever the opportunist, Temujin approached the Jin frontier commander with an offer: "I'll take care of those Tartars and subdue the Ongud tribe for you."

The Chinese commander agreed, and the coalition army of Jin and Mongols crushed the Tartars. For Temujin, this was vengeance for his father's death. He also amassed staggering treasure from the loot.

At this point, Toghril arrived. The two commanders allied against their common enemies, starting with the Merkits, who had regained strength. Temujin had a young man in his army named Subutai (Subedei) who was from the "reindeer country" (northern Russia). Although unschooled in horsemanship and Mongol warfare, Subutai was a genius at strategy. As a non-Mongol, Subutai managed to infiltrate the Merkit camp and spy out their battle plans. The Mongols pulverized the Merkits, and Temujin made Subutai a general and his master strategist.

In 1199 CE, Temujin and Toghril attacked the Naiman people of western Mongolia, who outnumbered the Mongols. At this point, Temujin and Jamuga formed an uneasy truce to fight the Naiman people. The timing would never be better, as the Naiman ruler had just died, and his sons were engaged in civil war.

However, when it was time to ride out to battle, Jamuga was missing in action. Temujin and Toghril fought through the day, defeating one Naiman prince before nightfall. When Temujin awakened the next morning, he was shocked that Toghril and his men had slipped away during the night. Jamuga had snuck in and convinced Toghril to abandon Temujin. The tables swiftly turned for Toghril when the other Naiman prince, Koksu-Sabrak, chased him down, killing or enslaving half of Toghril's army and capturing its cattle, food, and supplies. Toghril had to swallow his pride and go to Temujin.

Despite Toghril's desertion, Temujin needed Toghril's Keraite tribe to keep the Naiman people in check. He sent his top generals after the Naiman army. They arrived in time to save Toghril's son, Ilkha, from destruction and recaptured the stolen cattle.

Temujin and Toghril were a team again, facing off against the Merkits and Tayichiud, who had just allied. Temujin defeated their coalition forces, executed their nobles, and captured thousands of their women and children. However, Toghril's brother conspired against him and forced him into exile in China.

With Toghril gone, Temujin's adversaries made their move. Fifteen tribes, including the Tayichiud, Merkit, and Ongud, formed a coalition to take Temujin down. They were led by Jamuga, their "gurkhan," or universal ruler. All of Mongolia was at war.

However, not everyone in the fifteen tribes was happy about the situation, especially Dai Sechen, Temujin's father-in-law. He and several others leaked valuable information about battle plans to Temujin.

"I need you now!" Temujin desperately messaged Toghril, who was sulking in exile. "Get back here!"

Reproduction of a 1278 Chinese painting of Genghis Khan[81]

Jamuga decided to attack Temujin before Toghril could return. However, he moved too fast, not waiting for all the allied tribes to gather. He rode into battle with only his men and some of the Tayichiud. Jamuga commanded his wizards to produce a storm to blow Temujin's army away. Yet, their magic went awry. The snowstorm enveloped Jamuga's forces, blinding them.

Toghril arrived just in time, and Temujin scored an epic victory in the Battle of Dalan Balzhut, scattering the rebel forces. Yet, a poisoned arrow struck Temujin in the neck, piercing his artery. One of his generals, Jelme, sucked out the poison as Temujin faded into unconsciousness. At midnight, he awakened and weakly asked for milk. Jelme snuck into the Tayichiud camp and stole milk for his commander.

Meanwhile, Jamuga's coalition was dissolving. The Tayichiud were no longer a threat. In 1203 CE, another Naiman confederation attacked, joined by Jamuga and the few remaining Merkit and Tartars. It even included Temujin's uncle and two brothers. Temujin swallowed his feelings of betrayal and focused on strategy. He outwitted the enemy's plans at every turn, displaying incredible versatility. His orders seemed odd, but his men had learned to follow them, aware of his keen instincts.

In this war, Toghril adopted Temujin as his son, making him the crown prince of the Keraite tribe. This deeply offended Seng Gum, Toghril's son, who talked his father into betraying Temujin. The Keraite army caught Temujin by surprise, but Seng Gum was injured in the ensuing fray, and Temujin slipped away. Shortly after, Temujin launched a surprise night attack on Toghril's camp. Toghril escaped, but a random Namaan soldier killed him days later.

Temujin's army swelled to sixty-six thousand warriors. Once again, Jamuga rallied the Merkits, Keraites, and Naiman people against him. In the 1204 Battle of Chakirmaut, Temujin arrayed his soldiers in a long front line called a "lake formation." Guessing he meant to outflank them, the Naiman people also stretched their soldiers out to face him. Temujin suddenly launched a frontal assault in a "chisel battle," breaking through the thinned enemy line. Jamuga snuck away, but Temujin killed every man on the enemy side.

Temujin captured a Merkit princess named Töregene, who married Ögedei, his oldest biological son. Decades later, when her husband died, Töregene became regent of the Mongol Empire. Temujin also attacked the Western Xia in 1205 CE, a Sichuan Chinese-Tibetan people who ruled northwestern China's Tangut Empire from 1038 to 1227 CE. They put up no defense, and he plundered their herds and left.

Temujin is pronounced Genghis Khan; painting by Rashid al-Din, a late thirteenth-century physician who wrote a history of the Mongol and Turkish tribes.[32]

By 1206 CE, Temujin had conquered all his adversaries and killed Jamuga. The Mongol tribes gathered at the Onon River, where the shaman Koko Chu pronounced Temujin "Genghis Khan," or "Universal Ruler." Temujin now ruled the entire Mongol tribe and the other steppe tribes in Mongolia. The great empire had begun.

What Set the Mongol Army Apart?

The Mongol army fought almost entirely on horseback, with composite bows as their primary weapons. The Mongols were incredibly tough soldiers, able to ride for days with little food or water. Their stocky horses were also rugged. Each Mongol warrior rode one horse and had spares, changing out when their mount got tired or injured.

The Mongols were innovative, highly adaptable military strategists. They embraced innovations, such as adopting gunpowder from China. They had a stellar communications network called the *örtöö* or *yam*, which used horseback couriers and relay stations. By frequently changing to a fresh mount, the couriers could cover a jaw-dropping distance in one day. This became especially essential when the Mongolian Empire expanded to two continents.

Mongol warriors often feigned retreats. They pretended to give up and raced off the field, with the enemy in hot pursuit. They would usually ride their horses up a hill, then suddenly swing around and attack their chasers from an uphill advantage. Another favorite tactic was luring their enemies into an ambush.

The Mongols used psychological warfare to instill fear in their enemies. When they won a battle, they would leave several enemy survivors behind to relay the cruel deaths the Mongols inflicted on their captives. Sometimes, they captured a city, killed every living soul, and then warned nearby cities that the same thing would happen to them if they did not surrender.

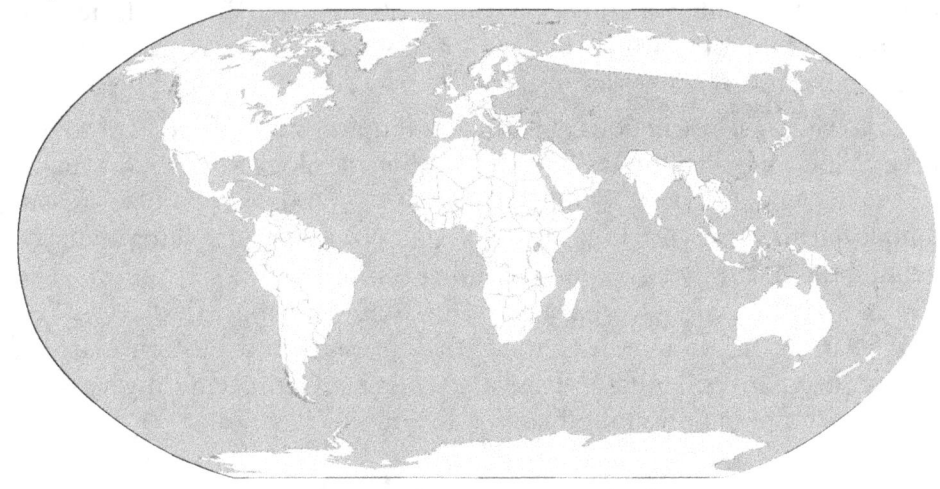

The Mongolian Empire at its height[38]

How Far Did the Mongolian Empire Extend?

After consolidating his leadership over the steppe tribes, Genghis Khan targeted China, attacking the Jurchen Jin dynasty in 1209 and 1211 CE. The Jin signed a peace treaty, agreeing to pay tribute to Genghis Khan. Yet, when they moved their capital south to Beijing (Zhongdu) in 1215 CE, he accused them of breaking the treaty and burned Zhongdu down. Genghis Khan also attacked the Western Xia in 1215 CE. After continued assaults by the Mongols, the Jurchen Jin state collapsed in 1234 CE. Genghis Khan did not live to see the great Mongol victory, having died in China in 1227 CE. His body was carried back to Mongolia and buried in a secret tomb.

Between campaigns in China, Genghis Khan targeted the Khwarazmian Empire, which covered today's Iran, Turkistan, and Uzbekistan. When he sent ambassadors demanding the shah become his vassal, the shah killed the ambassadors. Genghis sent a hundred thousand warriors into Persia, and the shah escaped to an island in the Caspian Sea. Genghis ruthlessly reduced city after city to ashes, killing men, women, and children. In 1221 and 1222 CE, he invaded today's Afghanistan and took control of the regions around the Caspian Sea.

Genghis Khan and his descendants had a reputation for massive destruction and abject violence. However, he allowed leaders to stay in power if they acknowledged him as their overlord and paid tribute. He also showed religious tolerance to Buddhists, Christians, Muslims, and other faiths. Genghis Khan established the Yassa, an unwritten law code that promoted unity, obedience to authority, and harsh punishment of anyone stepping out of line. He rewarded loyalty by elevating people of humble origins to high positions.

Following his instructions, his mighty empire was divided among his three living sons after he died, with his oldest biological son, Ögedei, as the next "great khan." Genghis Khan's grandson, Kublai Khan, conquered the rest of China in 1279 CE—collapsing the Song dynasty, creating the Yuan dynasty, and declaring himself China's emperor. The Mongols also invaded Korea, Japan, Pakistan, and the Middle East. At their peak in the thirteenth century, they pressed into Eastern Europe, conquering parts of today's Russia, Armenia, Georgia, Hungary, and Ukraine, stopping only at the Danube River.

Hulegu, Genghis Khan's grandson, and his wife, Doquz Khatun, Toghril's granddaughter. [84]

The Mongol Empire played an extraordinary role in connecting the East and West before it dissolved in the mid-1400s. One empire ruling such an astonishing swathe of the world enabled knowledge and technology to transfer freely. Protected trade routes encouraged cultural and economic exchange along the Silk Road.

Chapter 6: The Aztec Empire

Aztec folklore, written on picture books called codices, said the Mexica-Aztecs were one of seven Aztec tribes that emerged from seven caves in Colhuacan Hill on the idyllic island of Aztlan. The other six tribes had already crossed over the Lake of the Moon to the mainland. Yet, the Mexica remained in their peaceful paradise, where snowy white herons graced the shoreline, and ducks and large fish were easily caught in the sparkling lake water. No one ever grew old in Aztlan.

The seven caves on Aztlan; illustration from the Historia Tolteca-Chichimeca[85]

However, something mysterious and unexplained impelled them to leave their life of ease. When they crossed the lake, a hummingbird sang to them each night. It was Huitzilopochtli, the god of the sun and war:

"You are my people now. I will lead you to your new home and give you the tools you need for your journey," Huitzilopochtli said. "I will sing to you at night with instructions. You will become preeminent and prosperous, ruling over the other tribes. Yet, I require one thing in exchange: human sacrifice."

Xiuhcoatl, the Turquoise Serpent, was wielded by Huitzilopochtli against evil forces[66]

The Mexica-Aztecs eventually ruled eighty thousand square miles of central Mexico from their spectacular city built on an island in a swamp. Tenochtitlan, their capital, was among the world's largest cities from the fourteenth to the sixteenth century CE. It presided over five hundred city-states with six million people from multiple tribes. The Mexica created a sophisticated society with advanced agriculture, complex social hierarchy, and vibrant—albeit depraved—social practices.

What Happened as the Mexica Migrated from Atzlan to the Valley of Mexico?

After leaving Atzlan, the Mexica captured two men and a woman from the Chicomóztoc-Mimixcoa tribe and sacrificed them, laying their bodies across two cacti and a bush. Then, they traipsed through the harsh Mexican desert in a land turned against them. Thistles and thorns tore their skin, and poisonous lizards and snakes slithered across their path.

The first sacrifice, from the Codex Boturini[87]

When the Mexica finally reached the Valley of Mexico, their Aztec relatives and other tribes had already settled around Lake Texcoco, which covered over two thousand square miles. The Mexica had to carve out a place for their tribe. They hired themselves out to the other tribes as construction workers and mercenary soldiers. They made strategic marriages to build up allies.

The Colhuacan tribe gave the Mexica land to settle in exchange for military service. But the Mexica quickly wore out their welcome. After winning a stunning battle against the Xochimilca tribe, they asked the Colhuacan king for his daughter so they could worship her as a goddess. The chief was horrified to discover that the Mexica concept of worshiping her involved killing and skinning the young woman. He arrived at their village to find a priest wearing his daughter's skin!

The enraged Colhuacans drove the Mexica out. No one else wanted the macabre Mexica around either. The Mexica had to creep around, hiding in the mosquito-ridden swamps, trying to scavenge for food. When all hope seemed lost, Huitzilopochtli spoke to a Mexica priest in a dream: "In the morning, look for a prickly-pear cactus growing among the reeds. You will see an eagle perched on it, with a snake in its claws. That is where you will settle down and build your city, Tenochtitlan. From there, you will conquer all your enemies."

The following day, the Mexica set off in search—and there it was! On an island on Lake Texcoco's western shore was a prickly pear cactus with an eagle sitting on it, holding a snake in its talons. They laughed and cried. It was 1325 CE, and their forefathers had left Aztlan almost 150 years earlier. Now, they had an island for a new city and a bright future.

Mexico's coat of arms features an eagle on a cactus holding a snake. [88]

How Did Tenochtitlan Grow into a Sprawling Metropolis?

A bog sounds like an odd place for a new city, but the Mexica-Aztecs made it work. They had abundant fish and waterfowl. The Mexica used chinampas, or floating gardens, to grow corn, beans, and squash. The chinampas had underwater wooden stakes supporting woven reed platforms on the lake's surface. The Mexica dredged fertile mud from the lake bottom and piled it on the platforms, where they grew their produce.

The farmers paddled canoes around their floating gardens, and they could stand on the platforms to plant or harvest. In the warm lake region, they could grow multiple crops each year. Just south of Tenochtitlan was a waterway connecting Lake Texcoco to Lake Xochimilco, with more extensive floating gardens.

The Mexica-Aztecs built a gleaming city of adobe brick houses, palaces, and temples on their island. Instead of roads, they had canals, which they navigated by canoe. In the city center was the lavish Templo Mayor, the city's main religious center. It was a pyramid topped by two temples, one for Huitzilopochtli and the other for Tlaloc, the rain god. Glistening palaces for the city's nobility encircled the temple complex. Around the temples and palaces were four residential districts housing 200,000 people. Few European cities in the 1300s to 1500s were larger than Tenochtitlan, and they certainly were not as clean!

When the Spaniards arrived, they noticed how pristine Tenochtitlan was. It had an advanced waste management system, and its citizens kept the streets and their homes spotless. Dams and dikes provided flood control, and since the water around the city was slightly saline, an aqueduct brought in fresh drinking water. Causeways connected the city to the mainland.

Mural of Tenochtitlan by Diego Rivera [30]

What Was Remarkable about the Aztec Social and Economic Structure?

Aztec society had clearly defined social levels, with nobility, priests, and military commanders at the top. The second level included merchants, architects, and artisans. The third level was farmers and laborers, and at the bottom were enslaved people.

All young teens in Tenochtitlan, both boys and girls, attended school. The boys lived in dormitories and learned military arts. The upper-class boys also studied reading, writing, astronomy, and religion. The working-class boys studied religion and honed their skills in a trade. Teen girls learned dancing, singing, and theology at day school. Some learned medical arts, like midwifery.

Most enslaved people were war captives or people sent as tribute from conquered city-states. Occasionally, Aztec citizens sold themselves into slavery if they got into deep debt. The destiny of some enslaved people was human sacrifice, as the Aztecs sacrificed thousands of adults and children each year. Enslaved children were usually household servants, while enslaved males did farm and construction work. The educated often managed their owners' businesses. Enslaved people were rarely resold and could buy their freedom.

Most Aztecs were farmers who also fought in the military between the planting and harvest seasons. Additionally, farmers helped build temples, roads, and water systems in the off season. The Aztecs had complex irrigation canals, diverting water from rivers and lakes. In addition to farming the floating chinampas, they built terraces up the sides of mountains for planting.

The Aztec artisans had large workshops for carpentry, metalworking, ceramics, stone carving, and other skilled crafts. Since the Aztecs were almost constantly at war, they made many weapons, such as six-foot-long blowguns. They dipped blowgun darts in poisonous secretions from the skin of the Colorado River toad and the Mexican tree frog. Artisans also made war clubs embedded with razor-sharp obsidian, a black volcanic rock.

Some artisans were boat builders, as the Aztecs needed canoes to navigate around their canal city of Tenochtitlan and travel to other cities via the lake and river systems. The Aztecs had engineers and skilled craftsmen designing and building their aqueducts, dikes, canals, and causeways.

The traders and merchants were the fastest-growing class in Aztec society. They were becoming so rich and powerful that they might have upended the Aztec social system if the Spaniards had not arrived and disrupted everything.

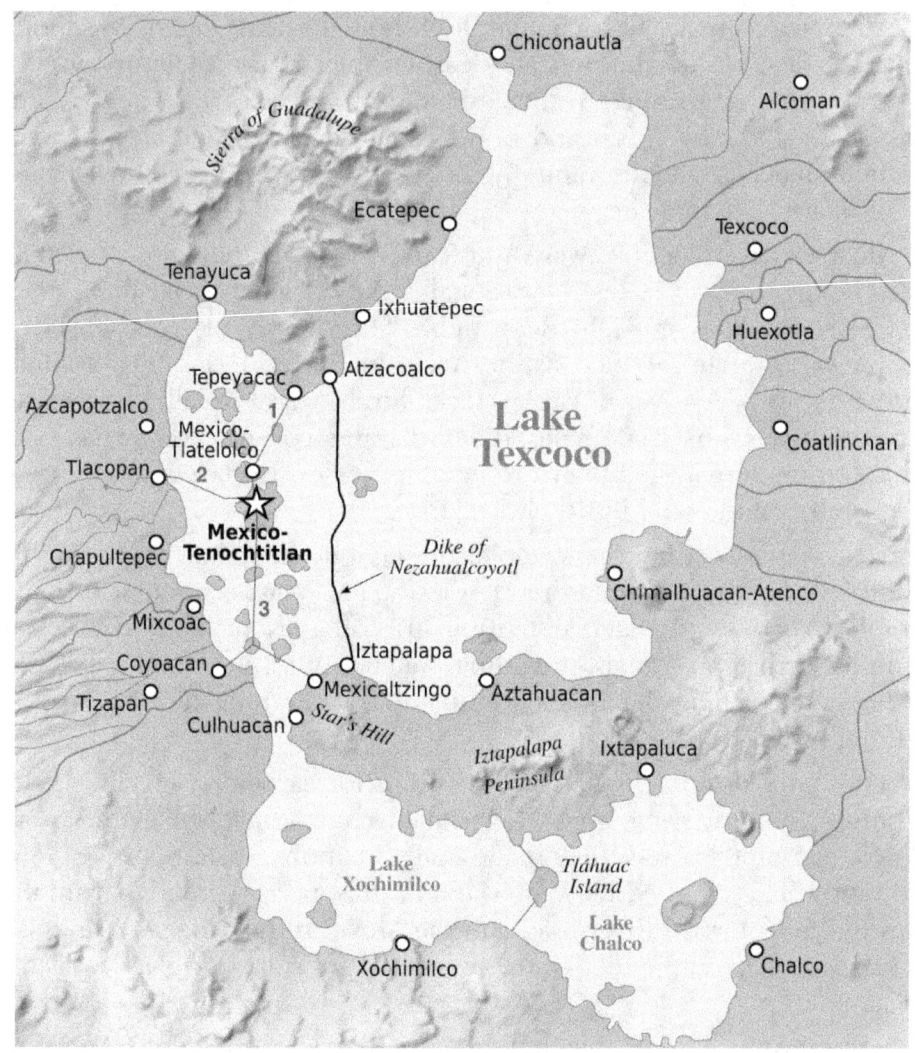

Cities around Lake Texcoco in the Aztec Empire[40]

After building Tenochtitlan in the southern marshes of Lake Texcoco, the Aztecs soon controlled most of the cities around Lake Texcoco. (Today, the lake is drained, and Mexico City sprawls over the region.) Through military conquest and strategic alliances, the Aztec Empire ultimately stretched from the Gulf of Mexico to the Pacific Ocean and reached south to Guatemala's rainforests. The conquered people enriched the empire through tribute, usually products made or grown in their region. Aztec merchants traded in goods from around the empire, like cotton cloth, precious gems and metals, featherwork, rubber, exquisite carvings, and brightly colored bird feathers.

How Did the Aztecs' Religion and Mythology Shape Their Culture?

The Aztecs worshiped many of the same gods as other Mesoamericans (people in the area from central Mexico to Costa Rica). The exception was their chief deity, Huitzilopochtli, the hummingbird god of the sun and war. Only the Aztecs worshipped him until they started building their empire. They forced conquered people to build temples to Huitzilopochtli but allowed them to continue worshiping other gods.

The Aztecs also adopted the deities of nearby civilizations. Their second-most important god was Tlaloc, the fanged, goggle-eyed rain god that virtually everyone in Mesoamerica worshiped. Huitzilopochtli demanded human sacrifice in increasing numbers, and so did Tlaloc. Yet, Tlaloc wanted children. About 20 percent of Aztec baby boys were drowned in the worship of the rain god.

The myth of the "Fifth Sun" was the Aztec creation story. The gods had to create a world, a sun, and people. Huitzilopochtli and his brother, Quetzalcoatl, created the first world. Its people were acorn-eating giants. Another brother, Tezcatlipoca, volunteered to be the sun. However, he was the smoke and mirrors god of darkness, so he did not shine brightly. The new world was always dim.

"This is no good!" the other gods muttered.

A turquoise mask of Tezcatlipoca"

Exasperated, Quetzalcoatl threw his club at Tezcatlipoca, knocking him out of the sky. He fell into the ocean and shapeshifted into a jaguar who ate the giants, ending the age of the first sun.

Now, it was Quetzalcoatl's turn to be the sun. He created people who ate pine nuts, and his sun shone brightly. Sadly, his people stopped praying. They became corrupt, greedy, and violent. Tezcatlipoca got his revenge on Quetzalcoatl by blowing all the people away in a hurricane. The survivors turned into monkeys and lived in the jungle.

In the third world, Tlaloc was the sun. This time, the humans prayed and lived morally. Unfortunately, while Tlaloc was giving light and warmth to the earth, Tezcatlipoca stole his wife. Heartbroken, Tlaloc forgot to send rain to his world. In desperation, the people prayed for rain, but Tlaloc ignored them. The harvest failed, and the starving people screamed out to Tlaloc. Tlaloc's grief turned to rage. "Here's your rain!" he snarled. Instead of water, he rained fire down on the earth, burning up the people. The survivors turned into turkeys.

Tlaloc's new wife, Chalchiuhtlicue, was the sun in the fourth world. She shone benevolently over the people. Yet, Tezcatlipoca, the troublemaker, played on her emotions: "Ha! You're pretending to love the humans, but you don't know what love is!" Deeply hurt, Chalchiuhtlicue began to cry. She was the water goddess, so her tears became rain. She kept weeping, and the rain caused a flood that swept over the earth, covering the mountains and drowning the turkeys. The surviving people morphed into fish to survive. Chalchiuhtlicue fell to the earth.

The gods were remorseful. "Our infighting has destroyed four worlds!" they cried. Quetzalcoatl and Tezcatlipoca apologized and transformed into giant oaks that pushed the sky back into place. The gods gathered around a great fire, discussing how they would create the fifth world. "Someone must sacrifice themselves to become the new sun!" they decided.

Tecuciztecatl, handsome yet vain, volunteered to jump into the bonfire. But he kept losing his nerve. Then, the ugliest and smallest god, Tonatiuh, leaped into the fire. Suddenly, the gods looked up to see a radiant new sun lighting the sky. Their cheers made Tecuciztecatl jealous. He finally got the nerve to leap into the fire. A minute later, two suns shone side by side.

"We can't have two suns!" grumbled one god. He snatched a rabbit and threw it at Tecuciztecatl. When the rabbit hit the second sun, Tecuciztecatl turned into the moon, with the imprint of the rabbit on his face. Now, only Tonatiuh shone as a brilliant sun; however, he was so frail he could not move across the sky. The other gods sacrificed their blood to give him the strength to orbit through the galaxy. Thus, for the Aztecs, sacrifice was imperative to maintain cosmic order.

This replica of the Sun Stone is painted in its original colors. "

In 1790, while repairing the Mexico City Cathedral (built over the Aztec Templo Mayor), workers discovered a twelve-foot-wide stone disk buried in the rubble. The Aztec Sun Stone had intricate carvings illustrating Aztec cosmology. Rays spread out from the sun god Tonatiuh, grimacing in the center. Four images representing the first four suns surround him. Further out on the disk is a circle of twenty glyphs (pictographs) representing the twenty days in an Aztec month. The glyphs on the outer ring relate to the solar calendar.

How Did Cortés and the Spanish Conquistadors Defeat the Aztec Empire?

In 1517 CE, the Spaniards discovered Mexico's Yucatan Peninsula when a storm blew one of their ships off course. Two years later, Hernán Cortés sailed eleven ships to the area to explore. After fighting the Maya in the Yucatán, he sailed north along Mexico's Gulf Coast, picking up several translators, including a shipwrecked friar. When the Spaniards arrived in Aztec territory, the Aztec Emperor Moctezuma sent them gold, politely asking them to go away. That did not work. Cortés only wanted more gold. He marched inland with his army, horses, and cannons.

Despite never having seen horses or cannons, the Aztecs were fearless warriors determined to fight for their empire. The Spaniards met other tribes—the Totonacs and Tlaxcalans—as they traveled inland to the Aztec capital of Tenochtitlan. Cortés convinced these tribes to ally with him against the Aztecs. These tribes hated the Aztecs for sacrificing their children and demanding heavy tribute payments.

In 1519 CE, Cortés met Moctezuma on the causeway leading to the island city of Tenochtitlan. The Aztec emperor cordially hung flowers and a gold chain around the conquistador's neck. Yet, Cortés had his guard up. Several days later, after learning that the Aztecs had attacked his men whom he had left at the coast, Cortés placed Moctezuma under house arrest.

Open war broke out a few months later when nineteen more Spanish warships arrived carrying fourteen hundred soldiers. Two thousand Tlaxcalans fought on the Spanish side. Moctezuma was killed in mysterious circumstances, and the Aztecs made his brother Cuitlahuac their new emperor. On La Noche Triste, or Night of Tears, the Spaniards and their Tlaxcalan allies fought a desperate and losing battle on the causeway leading out of the city. They lost about a thousand Spaniards and twice as many Tlaxcalan warriors.

Cortés spent the next few months convincing the other city-states around Lake Texcoco to ally with him against the Aztecs. Smallpox, brought to the New World by the Spaniards, hit Tenochtitlan in September 1520 CE, killing many warriors and the new emperor. The Aztecs made the emperor's cousin, Cuauhtémoc, their next (and last) emperor.

While the Aztecs fought smallpox, Cortés built thirteen small ships armed with cannons to launch a naval battle against Tenochtitlan. In April 1521 CE, his new ships sailed down a secret canal into Lake Texcoco. Meanwhile, a Spanish battalion cut the aqueduct bringing fresh water to the city. Five hundred Aztec canoes surged out of the city toward the new ships, but the Spaniards hoisted their sails and crushed any canoes that could not move out of the way fast enough. Ten thousand Tlaxcalans blocked the causeways leading to the island city, keeping other Aztec cities from joining the battle.

The Spaniards launched cannonballs at Tenochtitlan while the Aztecs shot a hail of arrows at their ships. Tenochtitlan's conquest took months. The Spaniards worked their way through the city, taking a section, burning it down, and then retreating to the causeways or their ships at night. The people in the city had no fresh water or food other than what their allies smuggled in by canoe in the dead of night. Finally, the starving remnant of Aztecs in Tenochtitlan surrendered, only to be viciously attacked by the Tlaxcalans. The Spaniards captured Emperor Cuauhtémoc and his family on August 13, 1521 CE, ending the Aztec Empire.

Chapter 7: The British Empire

How did a modest island nation become history's most extensive empire? What profound influence did Britain have on the world in those four centuries, beginning in the late 1500s? This chapter explores the economic ambitions, naval prowess, and political strategies that propelled Britain to establish colonies around the globe. The British Empire's complex legacy included cultural changes, the global spread of the English language, and new government systems.

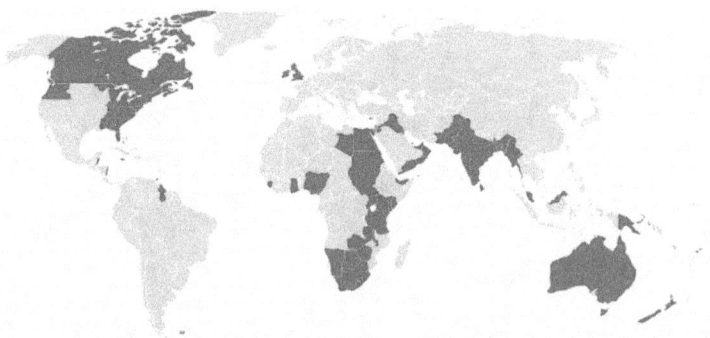

All the territory that was once part of the British Empire [48]

What Were the First British Colonies in the New World?

In 1603, when Queen Elizabeth I died, Great Britain was not great geographically. It was only England and Wales. A century would pass before Scotland officially united with Britain and two centuries before Ireland did the same. Yet, Britain had already begun building an empire in the New World, jumping into competition with Spain, Portugal, and France. Its first attempt failed in 1590 when 117 people mysteriously disappeared from Roanoke Island (North Carolina). A 1604 attempt to settle Guyana in South America also fizzled.

Britain founded its first permanent colony at Jamestown (Virginia) in 1607. One of its leaders was John Smith, who had been captured and enslaved by the Turks. After escaping, he joined the expedition to Virginia, only to be captured again, this time by the Powhatan tribe. Their chief planned to kill Smith, but the chief's daughter, Pocahontas, intervened. The Powhatan tribe helped the colonists survive the first brutal winter.

In 1609, the British ship *Sea Venture* was sailing to Jamestown with supplies and new colonists. A hurricane drove it off course and onto Bermuda's reef. Several British men stayed in Bermuda, establishing a permanent colony on Smith's Island. Using local cedar and the *Sea Venture*'s wreckage, the British built two ships and sailed to Jamestown with 137 people in 1610. They found only 61 colonists still alive.

The Puritans arrived in the New World in 1620, seeking freedom from religious persecution in England. They had a land patent to settle at the mouth of the Hudson River; however, winter gales blew the ship north to Cape Cod (Massachusetts). While pledging loyalty to King James I, they formed the Mayflower Compact, granting themselves self-government. At the Plymouth Colony, they elected their leaders and made their own laws.

In 1634, England's persecuted Roman Catholics settled the Province of Maryland. The Puritans founded Rhode Island in 1636 as a place where everyone could enjoy religious tolerance. In 1639, the Congregationalists, who followed a Reformed, Calvinist faith, settled Connecticut. And, in 1664, the British captured the Dutch colony of New Amsterdam and renamed it New York.

In the West Indies, Britain established colonies in St. Kitts (1624), Barbados (1627), Nevis (1628), and Jamaica (1655). Sugarcane plantations on the islands brought phenomenal wealth to Great Britain. At first, these colonies used indentured servants to farm plantations. Toward the end of the seventeenth century, they began importing African enslaved people.

How Did the British East India Company Impact India and China?

The British East India Company (EIC) controlled half of the world's trade in the 1700s. Incorporated under Queen Elizabeth I, it operated in India, Pakistan, Bangladesh, China, Persia, and Indonesia from 1600 to 1874. The EIC wielded both economic and political power over these nations. It had its own navy and an army twice as big as Britain's full-time army. The British East India Company built staggering wealth by importing cotton, tea, and spices to London. However, one-third of its employees died from tropical diseases, battles with pirates, and violent uprisings in India.

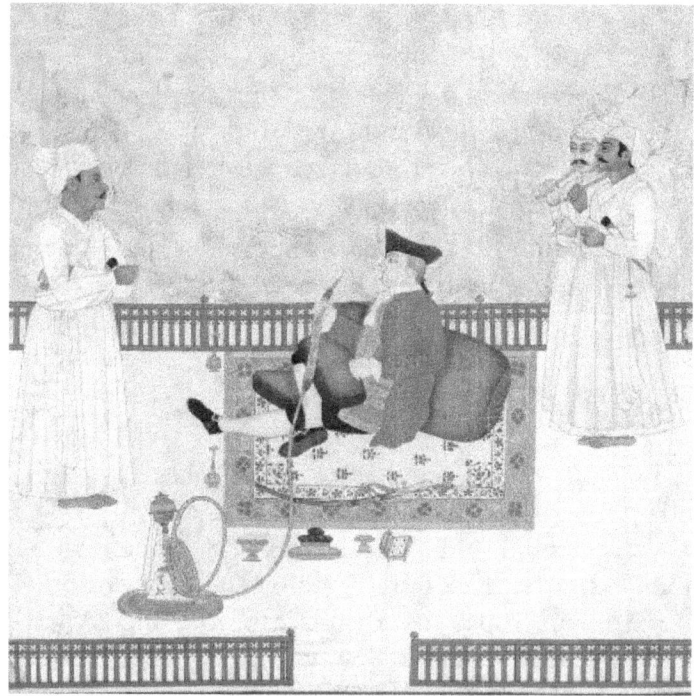

William Fullerton, an East India Company official, receiving a visitor "

Babar, a descendant of Genghis Khan, conquered northern India in 1526. Two hundred years later, his Mughal Empire ruled most of India. The Mughal emperor permitted the East India Company to set up trading posts. In the beginning, the relationship enriched both India and Britain. However, in the early 1700s, the Mughal Empire began to weaken. The East India Company capitalized on that by allying with local rulers to take control.

Soon, the East India Company ruled some of India's cities, like Bombay, Calcutta, and Madras. It was collecting taxes, minting coins, building forts, and running the police forces and justice systems. In 1784, the British Parliament passed the "India Act," giving the EIC control of trade and day-to-day affairs in these regions. Essentially, the EIC was a branch of the British government, especially since about one hundred members of the British Parliament were employees of the EIC.

China was the only country exporting tea then, and Britain wanted trade control. China had banned the import of opium because its recreational use had evolved into a horrific addiction issue. Britain flouted Chinese law by smuggling opium from India to China in exchange for tea and fine porcelain. China cracked down harder, and Britain responded by sending in warships and taking over Hong Kong in 1841.

By 1858, the British East India Company ruled most of India, Pakistan, and Bangladesh. This quickly changed when the Mughal Empire collapsed that year. The British East India Company had about 45,000 British troops and 230,000 Indian soldiers called "sepoys." These disgruntled Indian soldiers led the Sepoy Mutiny against the EIC. The British won, but it spelled the end of the EIC. The British government dissolved the East India Company in 1878 and ruled India directly until 1947.

Sepoy Mutiny "

What Was the Role of the Royal Navy in the British Empire?

James Thomson's poem, set to music, rallied the British around their navy as a key element to Great Britain's success as a world empire: "Rule, Britannia! Rule the waves: Britons never will be slaves."

The British Royal Navy did indeed rule the waves. It enabled Britain to become a global power, defend its interests, and move people, goods, and ideas across oceans. The navy's power at sea protected its merchant ships from pirates or attacks by ships of rival nations. It enabled supplies to reach British colonies and goods from the colonies to be shipped to England.

The British Navy's superiority gave Britain a decisive advantage over rival nations as it built its global empire. It spent more time on gunnery practice than other navies. Even when confronted by larger ships, the British Navy was impeccably trained in weaponry and seamanship. In 1675, a British clockmaker, John Harrison, invented the marine chronometer, immensely enhancing navigation through accurate longitude measurements.

How Did the Industrial Revolution Change the British Empire?

The British Industrial Revolution (1760-1840) was an era that experienced breathtaking technological breakthroughs. Exciting manufacturing, transportation, and communication inventions enabled the empire to thrive economically. New technology, like railways, steamships, and the telegraph, changed how people traveled and communicated. Large factories revolutionized world trade.

The invention of the power loom, spinning jenny, and water frame in the late 1700s radically changed cotton weaving. Previously, this was a time-consuming task done in homes or small workshops, all by hand. The fibers and seeds had to be separated, carded, turned into thread on a spinning wheel, and woven into cloth on a loom. These machines could do all this much faster. British factories imported the raw cotton from its colonies, wove it into cloth in factories in Britain, and then exported it worldwide.

Radical changes to the textile industry were not the only advances. Steam engines became much more efficient, requiring less fuel. Factories used stationary steam engines to run machines. Factory furnaces began using coke, a processed form of coal, especially for iron production. Technological advances fueled the British Empire's economic dominance, industrial growth, and global influence.

A London neighborhood near a factory, by Gustave Doré, 1870 ⁴⁶

The Industrial Revolution changed the demographics of Great Britain (and many other nations). With the boom in factory jobs in cities, people left their rural farm communities. Cities like Manchester, Birmingham, Glasgow, London, and Newcastle swelled in population. As people's income and standard of living increased dynamically, Britain's population tripled. Yet, there was a downside. City living was cramped, and the air near the factories was polluted. Diseases like typhus and cholera spread easily due to poor sanitation.

Women, who traditionally worked from home, went to work in the factories in droves. So did children—as young as eight. The factories paid women and children less yet preferred them because their small, nimble hands could work some machines better. Half of the textile factory workers were women, and half of Britain's school-aged children worked in the factories. Men, women, and children worked twelve-hour shifts until 1847, when it changed to ten-hour shifts.

In the colonies, the focus became mining or growing products like sugar, cotton, or tobacco. These raw products filled ships sailing to Great Britain's factories. Most colonies lacked the resources or technical knowledge to build their own factories with complicated machines.

What Were the Social and Cultural Dimensions of the Empire?

The British Empire facilitated the global spread of the English language, legal systems, education, and Christianity. By the late 1700s, English was spoken throughout the British colonies. In North America, it became the dominant language. In the Asian and African colonies, many people were bilingual, speaking English and their native language. Schools in the colonies taught the English language, and most taught other subjects like math and science in English. English was the language of trade, technology, and science.

The advantage of the global spread of English was that the world had a common language. Even after the British colonies gained independence, they continued using English as an official language. Today, English is written and spoken by more people than any other language in world history.

The British legal system also spread throughout Great Britain's colonies. The Royal Proclamation of 1763 said all British colonies had to follow English common law. However, places like Quebec and India already had legal systems. Local officials often tailored the British law to align with their existing legal systems.

Most of the earliest schools in Britain's Asian and African colonies were missionary schools. One objective was teaching children to read the Bible, and a second was educating Christian students to lead new churches in their region. A third objective was to educate the general population and lift them out of poverty.

As time passed, the British government began establishing standard schools in its colonies. Many taught basic reading, writing, and math but focused on developing practical skills. Usually, only students from elite families or exceptionally bright students received higher education. However, this was also true of students in Britain.

The British encountered diverse religions in its colonies, like Hinduism in India, Islam in the Middle East, and indigenous religions in Africa. One goal of the British rulers was to spread the Protestant

Christian faith. They sent missionaries and gave special privileges to folks who converted. This was especially the case in Africa. The British thought that converting the Africans to Christianity was essential to civilizing them. They also wanted to end practices like witchcraft.

David Livingstone was a famous missionary in Africa. He was born in 1813 to a low-income family in Scotland and went to work in the cotton mills at age ten. Despite leaving school early, he read every book he could find on science, philosophy, medicine, and religion. Eventually, he received some formal training in theology and medicine. He became a missionary doctor and explorer in Central Africa, where he vigorously campaigned against the slave trade.

Most of the Middle Eastern Muslims and people of India refused to change their religion. The British mostly stopped trying to convert them. However, they did outlaw religious practices like *sati*, an Indian custom that expected widows to throw themselves on their husbands' funeral fire. Missionaries like Amy Carmichael built group homes for girls who escaped from the Indian *devadasi*. This was a custom of "marrying" little girls to a god and placing them in service to temples, where they were sexually exploited.

Amy Carmichael with children in her care[47]

How Did Independence Movements Resisting British Rule Play Out?

Britain's colonists in America and other points of the globe became increasingly irritated by what they considered unfair trade policies. The colonies were not allowed to set the prices on items they exported, like tobacco, gold, and cotton. They could usually only export goods to Britain, which set rock-bottom prices. Britain processed the raw goods, then sold them back to the colonies.

Adding insult to injury, Britain began taxing the American colonies on wine, coffee, and sugar to pay its debt from the Seven Years' War. The 1765 Stamp Act taxed documents in the colonies, including newspapers. The Americans seethed: "We have no seats in Parliament. This is taxation without representation!"

Britain continued passing new tax laws, which the Americans felt were unfair. An angry crowd in Boston threw snowballs at the British soldiers in 1770. The soldiers opened fire, killing five colonists. The colonists responded to the tax on tea by boycotting British tea. They grew herbal tea or switched to coffee, which became America's patriotic beverage at that time. Finally, a group of colonists dressed like Native Americans attacked the British merchant ships in Boston Harbor, dumping 342 crates of tea into the water. The British responded to the "Boston Tea Party" by closing Boston Harbor and taking over Massachusetts' elected government.

In 1774, delegates from the American colonies met in Philadelphia for the First Continental Congress. They decided to form their own military and adopt a Declaration of Rights. "We are entitled to life, liberty, and property!" they declared. The British responded in April 1775 by attacking Concord and Lexington, Massachusetts. This did not end well for them. The colonists trounced the British and chased them back to Boston. The American Revolutionary War had begun.

A year later, the American colonists ran the British out of Boston. The Continental Congress signed the Declaration of Independence on July 4, 1776. It said that the government must have the consent of the people being governed. If the government became destructive, the people had the right to change or abolish it.

However, the war was far from over. It dragged on for another fifteen grueling months. Finally, George Washington confronted the British general Charles Cornwallis in Virginia. With assistance from the French, the American colonists won the war and gained independence.

India's quest for independence continued despite losing the Sepoy Mutiny of 1857. Queen Victoria, proclaimed Empress of India in 1876, tried to fix some of the issues. She promised the Indians equal opportunity in public service and that they could join the civil service. She also said she would stop taking land from the native princes and that India would have religious freedom. Nevertheless, she increased the number of British soldiers to outnumber the Indian soldiers in India's army. Furthermore, only the British could shoot high-caliber guns.

Mahatma Gandhi, 1931 [48]

By 1900, India had an all-Indian congress, yet the Muslims felt they did not have enough of a voice. Still, they agreed with the Hindus on one thing—they did not like British rule. Mahatma Gandhi became the leader of the Indian National Congress in 1921. He encouraged peaceful resistance and civil disobedience against the British rather than violence. "Non-violence is a weapon of the strong," he taught. In 1942, the Indian National Congress launched the "Quit India" campaign. "Leave immediately!" they told the British. "Give India independence!" The British threw Gandhi and over 100,000 other nationalist leaders in jail, publicly flogging the protesters.

Eventually, the British agreed to independence in 1947. Yet, they did not think the Hindus and Muslims could peacefully live and rule together. The British split off the northeastern section of India, making it the Muslim country of Bangladesh. Millions of Hindus whose ancestral homes were in Bangladesh relocated to India. They trudged south with the possessions they could carry, passing Muslims who had also been uprooted and were moving to Bangladesh.

World War II (1939-1945) almost broke the British Empire. It devastated its military and left it drowning in debt. Britain had neither the money nor the manpower to resist the independence movements in its colonies. Ceylon (Sri Lanka) won independence in 1948, Burma (Myanmar) in 1948, and Libya in 1951.

In 1952, Princess Elizabeth and her husband, Philip, were in Kenya, touring the Commonwealth. Word came that her father had died, making Elizabeth the queen of Great Britain. The British Empire was already evolving into the "Commonwealth of Nations," an association of independent countries that had once been part of the empire. Twenty-five-year-old Elizabeth II became their symbolic monarch.

Queen Elizabeth II, Coronation Day

Some countries were still in the process of gaining independence. For several, it meant violent uprisings. Malaya and Ghana became free in 1957. In the 1960s and 1970s, Kenya, Nigeria, Jamaica, and the Caribbean territories won independence. Britain returned Hong Kong to China in 1997, officially ending the British Empire.

Chapter 8: The French Revolution and the Dawn of a New Era

The French Revolution brought profound upheaval, ending the French monarchy. This pivotal event transformed France and changed the course of global history. What ignited the revolution? How did social inequality, economic distress, and Enlightenment ideas all play a part? Who were the major players? This chapter unwraps how the revolution dismantled the old feudal order and paved the way for modern democratic principles.

What Was the State of French Society in the Late Eighteenth Century?

King Louis XVI of France came to the throne in 1774. His government had ingrained issues that seemed unfixable. The most significant problems were finances and social inequality. France had a rigid class structure called the "Three Estates": the Roman Catholic clergy, the nobility, and commoners. The commoners—ordinary working-class people—comprised 90 percent of France's population. They had no voice in government and suffered under crushing taxes. The other 10 percent, the Roman Catholic clergy and aristocrats, got tax exemptions and other social advantages.

France's population grew at an unusual pace in the 1700s. Medical knowledge had improved, so fewer babies died in infancy. Farming technology had also improved, and there were no prolonged dry spells in the first two-thirds of the century. This meant children and adults had enough food. The population increased by about 50 percent to roughly 28,000. France had more people than any other European country, yet about one-third of its population lived in poverty.

The middle-class commoners, the bourgeoisie, did not suffer as badly. They were the merchants, business owners, or more successful farmers. Some grew wealthy and powerful enough to challenge the aristocratic class. New political ideas were filtering in, making them question how things were done. They realized that the elite folks running the country were inept at management. Worse yet, the ruling class were unethical, arbitrary, and cruel.

Marie Antoinette, 1775, by After Jean-Baptiste André Gautier-Dagoty[50]

In 1770, France's fifteen-year-old dauphin (crown prince), Louis XVI, married the fourteen-year-old Marie Antoinette. She was from Austria, the daughter of the Holy Roman Emperor. It was a political marriage, meant to unite two countries that had been enemies in the Seven Years' War. Marie's mother, the Empress of Austria, expected her daughter to manipulate affairs in France to Austria's advantage.

In 1774, France's King Louis XV died of smallpox, making his grandson, Louis XVI, king and Marie Antoinette the queen consort. Shortly after, drought struck, followed by an intense hailstorm ruining the harvests. Several outbreaks of the viral Rinderpest disease killed over 200 million cattle in Western Europe. The price of bread skyrocketed, leaving the people angry and desperate. Workers went on strike, and rioters filled the streets. The French disliked their Austrian queen and accused her of gambling and reckless spending on lavish clothes and furniture. "We're starving, and she's draping herself in silk and diamonds!" they protested.

Why Was France in a Financial Crisis?

One reason France was in financial trouble was its mountain of debt, which grew to twelve billion livres by 1789. Louis XVI's grandfather had plunged the nation into debt through several European wars. After becoming king, Louis XVI got France involved in the American Revolution, initially as a secret supporter of the colonists. France sent clandestine supply shipments, beginning in 1776. Later, France formed a formal military alliance with the colonists, sending financial, military, and naval support to America.

Meanwhile, Louis XIV and his queen were overspending on fine clothing, an ostentatious lifestyle, and enlarging the opulent Versailles palace. Because France was so deeply in debt, it had to pay astoundingly high interest rates on loans. The interest rates and continuous spending made it almost impossible to repay the loans. Creditors began demanding repayment in the 1780s. Since the upper classes were exempt from taxes, the middle and lower classes carried the tax burden, leading to increasing unrest.

Hall of Mirrors in Versailles Palace [51]

Finally, the king's controller general, Charles-Alexandre de Calonne, recommended revising the tax code to include the wealthy aristocrats. In 1787, Calonne convened the Assembly of Notables to approve his reforms. However, the aristocratic Assembly refused to pass the reforms because they would have to start paying taxes. "We do not have the power to do this," they said. "Only an assembly of the Estates-General can pass legislation like this."

The Estates-General was a governing body of elected officials from three classes of society: clergy, nobility, and commoners. An Estates-General had not been called in 175 years, and it was not something Louis XVI wanted to do. For one thing, the Estates-General was more of an advisory council, not one that passed laws. It made recommendations to the king, who made the decisions and passed any laws. Louis XVI did not want to be in the position of passing an unpopular law that would bring down the wrath of the aristocrats. He fired Calonne and asked the parliaments to consider the tax reforms. In France at that time, aristocrats led thirteen parliaments, or courts. This group also refused to approve the tax reforms. "You must call an Estates-General!" they insisted.

Finally, King Louis called for the Estates-General of 1789. It had 282 representatives for the nobility, 303 for the clergy, and 578 for the "Third Estate," or the commoners. As the Estates-General met, its representatives were challenged by revolutionaries who wanted to turn society on its head. The revolutionaries wanted a new society built on the Enlightenment motto: "*Liberté, égalité, fraternité*" or "Liberty, equality, fraternity."

How Did the Enlightenment Thinkers Change Political Ideals?

The Enlightenment or Age of Reason (1685–1815) was a European movement that questioned old political traditions. It pushed logic, intellectualism, individualism, and science as the path to humanity's improvement. The Enlightenment thinkers' ideas about individual rights, separation of powers, and social contracts inspired people to challenge traditional authority and demand greater freedoms.

Voltaire was a French Enlightenment philosopher who advocated for social equality, freedom of speech, and religious tolerance. He was critical of the Catholic Church and France's absolute monarchy, both of which he believed held the people down. He promoted the separation of the church and the government.

Jean-Jacques Rousseau believed that people are good at their core, but the inequality and injustices of society corrupt their morality. In *The Social Contract*, Rousseau wrote that society should not have slavery and that people in a community should decide together on the common good. However, he believed in a strong government; otherwise, there would be chaos and no freedom.

Montesquieu taught the separation of powers into the executive, judicial, and legislative branches, which the American Constitution adopted. He warned that if a government becomes too authoritarian, it will essentially enslave the people. He promoted religious tolerance but believed "natural law" should prevail. He taught that the government must guarantee justice and freedom to everyone.

What Key Events Marked the Revolution's Beginning?

The Estates-General of 1789 was floundering. The Third Estate refused to verify the elections of the representatives, which had to happen before they could do anything. The Third Estate wanted individual voting, but the nobility refused to cooperate. They wanted a unified vote from each block of the "Three Estates." The nobility would get one vote, the clergy one, and the commoners one. Thus, the two votes from the nobility and clergy would outnumber the commoners' vote.

On June 4, King Louis's seven-year-old son died of tuberculosis, pulling the king away from involvement. The Third Estate began a roll call on June 13. Technically, they were not allowed to start proceedings without the king's permission and the agreement of the nobility and clergy. Nevertheless, the Third Estate plowed ahead. Four days later, they announced they were now the National Assembly. The clergy and nobility had no choice but to join them.

On June 30, everyone arrived at the assembly hall to find the door locked and guarded by soldiers. "Does King Louis plan to attack us?" they wondered.

Joseph-Ignace Guillotin cleared his throat. He was a physician and the secretary of the National Assembly. Several months later, he would develop the guillotine as a "painless" way of beheading people. "Does it matter where we meet? What about the royal tennis court? We can meet there."

The group nodded and gathered at the indoor tennis court. There, they swore the "Tennis Court Oath," which said the National Assembly could meet anywhere. "We will not disband until we give France a new constitution!" they declared.

King Louis XVI had been mourning his son but finally realized that matters were spiraling out of control. He had to take charge of the "revolutionary" National Assembly. Louis called up thirty thousand soldiers. The people of Paris were in a state of panic. Most supported the reform efforts of the National Assembly, yet rumors circulated that a military coup was imminent. "We need to arm ourselves!" the people warned each other.

Storming the Bastille [53]

On July 12, 1789, the Parisians rioted. In the "Storming of the Bastille," hundreds of people broke into Paris's fortress to get weapons and gunpowder. The French Revolution had begun. To quiet the crowds, King Louis disbanded his soldiers. Yet, the king's brother and other royalty escaped France on July 16. They feared what was to come.

Soon, all of France was in an uproar. The poor farmers revolted against their landlords and tax collectors, looting and burning their homes. France followed the feudal system of aristocratic "lords" owning the land and poor peasants (serfs) farming the land in exchange for "protection" from the lords and the right to keep a small portion of the harvest. The lords essentially "owned" the peasants, who had no right to leave the estate and find work elsewhere. On August 4, the National Assembly banned feudalism. They gave the serfs their freedom and stripped the wealthy landowners of their privileges.

Later in August, the National Assembly passed the Declaration of the Rights of Man and of the Citizen, which was based on Enlightenment thought. It presented a new government based on the people's will, with a representative government. It mandated the separation of powers and universal human rights like freedom of speech.

Writing a new constitution was far more difficult. It took two years to complete. The National Assembly had to hash out questions like how much authority the king would have. Several wondered if a king was even necessary. Meanwhile, Louis XVI was sullenly brooding in his palace. "I should have the right to a full veto of this new constitution!" he raged.

His lack of cooperation angered the ordinary people, especially the women. "We haven't enough bread, and this king refuses to cooperate!" they complained.

On October 4, 1789, a throng of wrathful women from the marketplace marched on Versailles, pounding drums and brandishing knives and sturdy sticks. Someone started ringing a church bell, and more people joined in, swinging by city hall to grab weapons and two cannons. They pressed on through a downpour and arrived at the palace, exhausted and dripping wet. The king had been hunting and got back to the palace just as the horde of citizens arrived. The women's spokesperson was a seventeen-year-old girl who fainted at the king's feet. He immediately knelt to help her, softening the agitated crowd.

"I'll have food sent to Paris from my royal stores!" he promised. He agreed to ratify the decree on feudalism and the Declaration of the Rights of Man.

In the dead of night, the national guard arrived, led by the French military officer Lafayette. He calmed down the people, then met privately with King Louis. "You'll be safer if you and your family return with me to Paris."

"I'll give you my answer in the morning," the king answered.

Yet, before dawn, attackers broke into the palace. "We'll tear the queen's heart out!" they yelled. They killed two guards and mounted their heads on pikes.

Marie Antoinette raced out of her room, barefoot. "Save my children!" she screamed.

Finally, the national guard managed to subdue the rioters, and the king agreed to accompany Lafayette back to Paris with his family. The unrest in Paris quieted, and relative peace reigned for the next year and a half. Yet, in June 1791, the king tried to sneak out of France with his family. They were caught and returned to Paris, but people began seriously discussing whether they needed a king. "Look!" they said. "The American colonists have established a republic with an elected president!"

The French people were divided. The Jacobins did not want a king at all. A second group, the Feuillants, wanted a constitutional monarchy with a king. However, they did not want him to hold absolute power.

In 1792, Austria and Prussia came to King Louis XVI's aid, no doubt worried that France's revolutionary ideas might spread. Furthermore, many of France's nobility had fled to those two countries for refuge and were demanding aid to get France back to the way it was. The French revolutionaries declared war on Austria and Prussia to squelch these counterrevolutionary efforts.

The guillotine, a symbol of the French Revolution [58]

France also had counterrevolutionaries at home. Thousands were massacred in the ensuing violence. In August, the Jacobins raided the palace and captured the king and queen. They put Louis XVI on trial for treason and high crimes against France. He was sent to the guillotine to be decapitated in January 1793. His queen met the same fate nine months later. Horrified, the Dutch Republic, Great Britain, and Spain joined Austria and Prussia in the war against France.

How Did the Reign of Terror Traumatize France?

With multiple factions trying to gain control, France descended into chaos. A radical faction of the Jacobins snatched control of the National Assembly. They issued a new calendar and outlawed Christianity, exiling 30,000 priests and sending hundreds more to the guillotine. Their Committee of Public Safety took almost total power over the government. It first halted the foreign armies on France's borders, then savagely pulverized the other factions in France vying for power.

Beginning in early 1793, a radical Jacobin named Maximilien Robespierre dominated the Committee of Public Safety for ten months. He led the grisly Reign of Terror, in which 16,594 men and women lost their heads at the guillotine. The committee even sliced the heads off sixty-six children.

Finally, the people revolted against Robespierre, sickened by the climate of fear and the daily executions. In July 1794, they sent Robespierre and his closest associates to the guillotine, ending the Reign of Terror. This led to the Thermidorian Reaction, in which the more moderate French people successfully focused on ending the war with other nations.

How Did Napoleon Bonaparte Rise to Power?

General Napoleon Bonaparte became France's hero when he trounced Italy and their Austrian allies in 1797. He staged a coup in 1799, making himself the consul of France, the top political leader. He ended the civil wars and many of the revolution's ideals. Napoleon focused on restoring stability to France, which had been traumatized by years of violence. He reformed France's education, banking, and legal systems.

His government passed a constitutional amendment in 1802, which made him consul for life. In 1804, he declared himself France's emperor and his realm the French Empire. Under his leadership, France dominated much of Western Europe. He met his downfall in 1813 when he attempted to invade Russia. The Russians lured him deep into the country, where he was unprepared for the harsh winter. He lost all but 100,000 of his 600,000-man army. Months later, a coalition force of Austrians, Prussians, Russians, and Swedes defeated him in eastern Germany. Napoleon abandoned his plans to conquer all of Europe and was forced into exile.

Amazingly, France wanted a king again, but this time in a constitutional monarchy. They made Louis XVI's younger brother, Louis XVIII, their new king. After several decades and two more revolutions, France abandoned the monarchy forever and established the French Second Republic.

What Were the Long-Term Impacts of the French Revolution?

The revolution abolished the feudal system, which had kept farmers in a semi-enslaved status for centuries, and set France on the path to democracy. The country underwent a series of transformations until it reached its Fifth Republic in 1958. The revolution also built a long-lasting pride among the French people in their national identity. It reshaped political boundaries and ideologies across Europe. The Roman Catholic Church had held considerable power over France's government, and this mostly ended. Although the French Revolution was a savage time, its ideals influenced other nations worldwide to move from absolute monarchies to more democratic governments.

Chapter 9: The Rise and Fall of the Soviet Union

The Soviet Union's history spanned over seven decades from the Bolshevik Revolution in 1917 to its dissolution in 1991. How did the desire for a classless society lead to the world's first socialist state under Lenin? What did subsequent leaders like Stalin do to consolidate power and expand the Soviet Union? How did the Cold War and the Space Race change the world? This chapter answers these questions and explores the events leading to the Soviet Union's collapse.

Why Were the Russians Unhappy with the Tsar?

Russia's people lived in deplorable conditions, and the strain of war made matters unbearable. Russia entered World War I in July 1914, allied with France and Britain against Austria-Hungary and Germany. Russia had a million-man army and four million reserves, yet they were not well trained. Russia's military technology and skill were lacking. Thus, jaws dropped when Russia invaded East Prussia and won the Battle of Stallupönen and the Battle of Gumbinnen on August 17 and 20.

However, Russia could not hold its edge. The two Russian generals leading the invasion hated each other and refused to communicate. They gave commands to their troops via radio, and the Germans had the technology to listen in. After pinpointing their location, the Germans shelled the Russian troops for a week, killing 120,000 soldiers and capturing 100,000. The Russians retreated in humiliation and dared not strike Germany again.

By April 1916, the mood in Russia was gloomy. Tsar Nicholas II was technically the supreme military commander but had never fought in a battle. General Brusilov wanted to attack Austria. He surprised everyone when his assault succeeded on its first day, netting him 26,000 prisoners. Ultimately, the Germans and Austrians lost over a million soldiers to Brusilov, with another 400,000 captured. However, the assault cost Russia more than a million men.

A Russian WWI poster [44]

In the east, German vessels attacked Russian ships and Black Sea ports. The Ottoman Empire was trying to snatch territory on the eastern side of the Black Sea. Russia lost another million men, leaving the people restless and irritated with their tone-deaf leadership. The Russians had long considered their tsars out-of-touch, unjust, and tyrannical.

Although Russia had eliminated serfdom in 1861, the farmers had to make payments to their former landlords. The payments and occasional bad harvests kept them close to starvation. When the Industrial Revolution struck Russia in the late 1800s, thousands of Russians moved into the cities to work in the factories. Moscow and St. Petersburg nearly doubled in population. Yet, the Russian factory workers lived in ghastly slums with low pay. The incessant poverty of Russia's population made them question their monarchy: "America and France both did away with their kings. Look how they are thriving now! What good is our tsar?"

In 1905, nine years before WWI started, a throng of Russians marched on the palace, insisting that the ordinary people have a voice in government. They demanded better living and working conditions. The tsar's guards opened fire, wounding or killing over a thousand. The Bloody Sunday Massacre led to more revolts and strikes as the factory workers, farmers, and soldiers demanded a say in the government.

Nicholas II agreed to form a Duma, a type of congress with elected leaders—a new thing in Russia. The tsar even agreed to include factory workers and farmers in the Duma. However, Nicholas's seeming support for the Duma melted away when it called for reforms. He disbanded the Duma and dissolved the next one that formed in 1907. The third Duma had only nobility and upper-class people; the fourth had better representation but hardly any power.

How Did the Bolshevik Revolution of 1917 Upend Russia?

The Russians were weary of war. Fighting on multiple fronts had cost them more men than any war in any country up to that point in history. The hard life of Russia's farmers and factory workers grew harder as WWI drove up the price of bread and fuel. The Marxist Bolshevik movement, led by Vladimir Lenin, capitalized on the people's felt needs. It promised "peace, land, and bread" for everyone.

In 1915, Tsar Nicholas made the irrational decision to travel to Mogilev (in modern-day Belarus) and take command of the Russian forces. He had no

Vladimir Lenin, 1917[65]

war experience, yet he hoped his effort would quiet the restless Russians. However, when Germany continued to crush the Russian troops, the blame fell on Nicholas. Both Nicholas and his wife were cousins of Wilhelm II, Germany's emperor. Whispers swirled that the tsar and his wife were secretly colluding with the Germans.

In early 1917, Russia's underdeveloped infrastructure collapsed. Trains that would normally bring grain to Russia's cities now transported troops and supplies to the front. The Germans and Turks blockaded Russia's Black Sea ports, cutting off fuel and other essential raw materials needed to operate the trains. Russia's people were starving and had no fuel for heat, while January temperatures hovered around 11°F (-12°C).

In February 1917, the fuming people of Petrograd poured into the streets, throwing bricks through bakery windows to steal bread. Tsar Nicholas was still in Mogilev as workers went on strike. "End the war! Dethrone the tsar!" they demanded.

In early March, police shot into the crowds, killing more than two hundred. This did not sit well with the Russian soldiers, who were primarily farmers and factory workers before the war. Ten thousand soldiers in Petrograd mutinied, marching with the protesters and burning down police stations.

Petrograd's soldiers fire on police in March 1917. [66]

Nicholas II knew his reign had ended. He started traveling home, but the journey took a week. Although warned to take her children and leave the country immediately, the tsarina waited for her husband to return.

When he did, they discussed their options. They hoped to flee to England, where their cousin, George V, was king. The British Parliament was willing to give them refuge, but King George feared political fallout. Britain desperately needed Russia's support in the war. Russia's new government was unlikely to continue allying with Britain if it took in their exiled tsar. Other European countries were equally hesitant.

The Bolshevik Revolution of October 1917 replaced Russia's monarchy with a Communist regime. Factory workers, farmers, and soldiers were in charge, and Lenin was its dictator. War raged between the Bolshevik "Red Army" and the "White Army." The White Army represented a hodgepodge of ideologies ranging from those who still wanted a tsar to those who wanted a different version of socialism than Lenin's. With civil war raging, Russia withdrew from World War I in March 1918. In July, the Bolsheviks shot and bayoneted Nicholas II, his wife, and all their children.

Russia's new Bolshevik government revolved around key principles of Karl Marx and Lenin. They believed a radical revolution that broke the capitalist system was necessary for their Communist utopia. Lenin believed a dictator should lead the country, acting on behalf of the proletariat (working-class people). Marxist-Leninists advocated for the working class to hold economic and political power, equal wealth distribution, and communal land ownership.

A woman named Fanny Kaplan viewed Lenin as a traitor to genuine socialism. She fired three shots from her pistol at Lenin in August 1918. One bullet punctured his lung, and another lodged in his shoulder. She was immediately executed, and the "Red Terror" was unleashed.

The Red Terror was a Bolshevik movement of extreme violence lasting from September 1918 to 1922 that aimed to crush any opposition. The Cheka (the Bolshevik secret police) had unprecedented powers to arrest and torture anyone they considered "anti-revolutionary." They executed people without a trial or sent them to the "Gulag," forced labor camps. The secret police not only targeted outspoken opponents but also religious leaders, intellectuals, and the former nobility.

What Draconian Polices Did Joseph Stalin Pass?

Joseph Stalin joined Russia's revolutionary movement in the 1890s, organizing protests and strikes. He impressed Lenin with his ruthlessness in the underground Bolshevik movement. Stalin was sent to a Siberian labor camp in 1910, but he escaped and helped with Lenin's revolution by publishing *Pravda*, the Bolshevik newspaper. After taking power, Lenin appointed Stalin as General Secretary of the Communist Party.

When Lenin died in 1924, Russia had collective leadership for several years. However, Stalin announced he was Lenin's political heir. Many expected Leon Trotsky, general of the Red Army, to be the next leader. Stalin used his power to exile Trotsky, and by 1929, he was the Soviet Union's dictator.

Russia lagged behind Western Europe in industrialization. Stalin instigated a series of five-year plans to modernize the Soviet Union, making its factories and farms more productive. He succeeded in increasing coal, steel, and oil productivity and stimulating economic growth in Russia. Yet, success came at a great price. If factories failed to meet their quotas, the workers were imprisoned or even executed.

When Russia did away with feudalism in the 1860s, it divided the large estates into small owner-operated farms. This system was in place when Stalin took power. Stalin instituted "collectivism," where the state took over the farms. The farmers rebelled against losing their farms. They hoarded grain and killed their farm animals, resulting in famines in which five million died. Stalin killed or imprisoned millions of farmers.

By the late 1930s, the government had consolidated all the small farms into large, state-owned collective farms. The government expected that introducing mechanized equipment and more organization would increase production. It set unrealistic harvest goals. When the goals were unmet, the government sent the grain and produce to the cities and the military. It did not allot any to the farm workers, and five million starved to death. Thousands of farmers left the rural areas to work in the cities.

A 1935 propaganda poster of Stalin [57]

Stalin promoted himself in the press and on posters plastered everywhere as the Soviet Union's all-powerful hero and its great, all-knowing leader. Poetry, statues, and hymns exalted him as if he had divine status. Yet, Stalin grew paranoid, fearful of potential opposition. From 1936 to 1938, Stalin's Great Purge wrecked the Soviet Union even further. He executed over half the Central Committee members and most of his highest military officers. His secret police enforced his Stalinist cult, killing 750,000 people and sending three million to Siberia's Gulag.

How Did the USSR Catapult to Superpower Status?

In August 1939, Stalin signed a secret pact with Adolf Hitler. They agreed not to fight each other and to divide Eastern Europe between them. At first, all went as planned. One week after signing the pact, Germany attacked Poland from the west. The next day, the Soviet Union attacked Poland from the east. The plan was for Germany and the USSR to divide Poland between them.

In 1940, still following the secret pact, Stalin annexed part of Finland, then moved on to take Estonia, Latvia, Lithuania, and part of Romania. Invading Romania broke the agreement with Hitler, and he reacted. The

Nazi blitzkrieg attack tore through Poland and into the USSR in Operation Barbarossa. It decimated the Russian army, leaving Stalin paralyzed with shock as Hitler's forces closed in.

Stalin gathered his wits and joined the Allies. In 1942, the epic Battle of Stalingrad began. "Not a step backwards!" Stalin warned his men. He lost over a million men but trounced the Nazis in 1943, pushing them out of Russia, out of Poland, and back into Germany. It was a turning point in WWII, shifting the balance of power from Hitler to the Allies. The Soviet Union now ruled a vast swathe of Eastern Europe, even the eastern half of Berlin, Germany's capital. The United States, France, and Great Britain occupied West Berlin.

After World War II ended in 1945, the Iron Curtain fell. The Soviet Union had allied with Britain, America, and the other Allies to beat Hitler. After the war, they were rivals in the "Cold War." Political and ideological barriers separated the democratic, capitalist nations and the USSR's totalitarian Communist state.

The Cold War heated up from June 1948 to May 1949 when the Soviets blocked land and water access to West Berlin. The "Berlin Blockade" was supposed to drive the Allies out. However, the Allies formed the "Berlin Airlift," which flew fuel, food, and medicine to the 2.5 million people in West Berlin. Finally, Berlin formally split into East Berlin and West Berlin and stayed that way, separated by a wall, until 1989.

The Soviet Union had become a superpower, ruling fifteen states and covering one-sixth of the globe's land mass. It was the world's largest nation, geographically.

What Were the Arms Race and Space Race All About?

The nuclear arms race and the Space Race exemplified the competition between the two superpowers. America wanted to keep the Soviet Union from annexing more nations. It built up its weaponry to unprecedented heights. After the United States dropped two atomic bombs on Japan in WWII, it continued developing nuclear weapons. The Soviet Union refused to be outdone. It had captured Nazi nuclear scientists when it invaded Germany. Now, the German scientists were helping the Soviet Union make its own bomb. The USSR tested "First Lightning" in Kazakhstan in 1949.

President Truman's response was to direct the United States's Atomic Energy Commission to develop the "superbomb," a hydrogen bomb. It uses both fused atoms and split atoms, making it a thousand times more lethal than an atomic bomb. The USSR dived into the race for the hydrogen bomb.

Meanwhile, the Soviet Union was enticing nations worldwide to become allies. The Korean War raged from 1950 to 1953, with China and the Soviet Union backing Communist North Korea, and the United States supporting South Korea. North Korea failed to unify the peninsula as a Communist nation.

Cuba had been friendly with its near neighbor, the US. However, Fidel Castro staged a Communist revolution in 1959 and allied with the Soviet Union. President Kennedy made an ill-fated effort to upend Castro's government by using exiled Cubans to invade the island. The Bay of Pigs invasion of 1961 was a fiasco.

This led to the Cuban Missile Crisis of 1962. The Soviets gave nuclear-armed missiles to Cuba, putting the eastern United States in imminent danger. A US reconnaissance pilot spotted the missiles, and President Kennedy huddled with his executive committee. Kennedy decided to blockade Cuba's waters and warned the Soviet Union to remove the missiles. Soviet vessels sailed close to the US Navy ships surrounding Cuba, yet they did not try to break the blockade.

Finally, Khrushchev, the Soviet Union premier, sent a message to Kennedy: "If you promise not to invade Cuba, I will remove my missiles." With the crisis averted, Kennedy and Khrushchev set up a hotline between their capitals and agreed to treaties on nuclear weapons.

In 1979, the Soviet Union sent troops into Afghanistan to support its fledgling Communist government against Islamic militants, the Afghan Mujahideen. The United States, Pakistan, and other nations supported the Mujahideen in the ten-year struggle. The war drained the Soviet economy and hurt it politically. It also devastated Afghanistan's infrastructure and culture. Atrocious human rights violations occurred on both sides. When the Soviet Union withdrew in 1989, it left a power vacuum, and civil war ensued. The Taliban, a radical Muslim group, took power.

The arms race played out alongside the Space Race as the Soviet Union and the United States competed in the final frontier. The Soviets won the first round in October 1957 when they launched Sputnik I. It was the first satellite to pass out of Earth's atmosphere. Sputnik traveled 139 miles from Earth's surface and circled Earth 1,440 times over three months. Aerodynamic drag finally pulled it out of orbit, and it fell back into Earth's atmosphere, where it burned up in the intense heat caused by denser air levels.

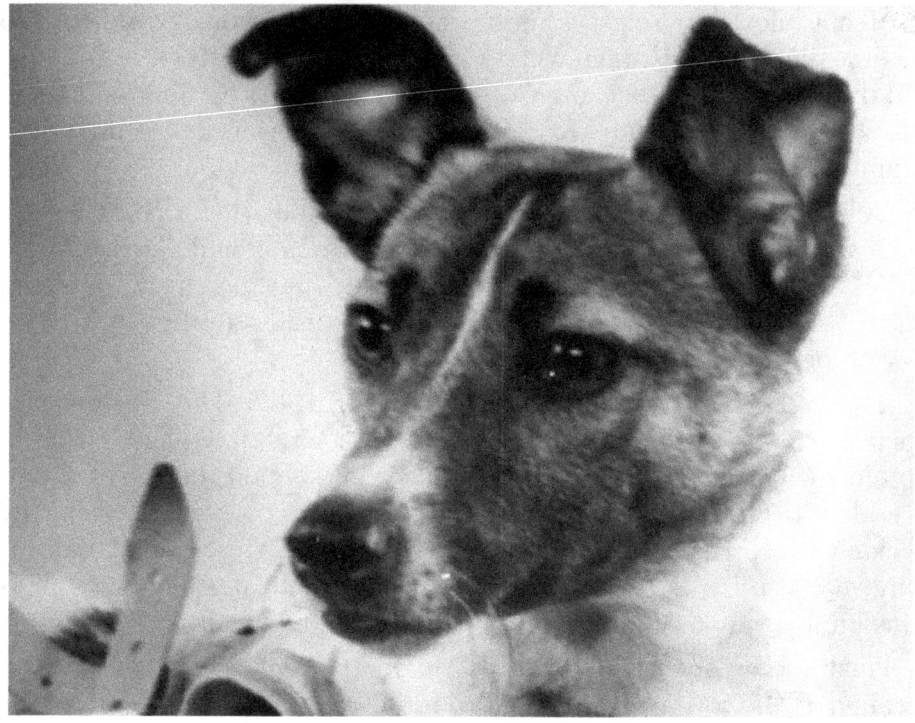

Laika the space dog [38]

The Soviets sent up Sputnik 2 a month later, this time with a passenger—a dog named Laika. The satellite's thermal system malfunctioned, and Laika overheated and died five hours into flight. However, Sputnik 2 orbited Earth for five months before it burned up on re-entry. Three months after Sputnik 2's launch, the US launched its first satellite into space, Explorer 1. The Soviet Union was also the first to send an unmanned rocket to the moon. *Luna 2* hit the moon at 7,400 miles per hour.

In April 1961, the Soviets sent the first man into space three weeks before the Americans sent Alan Shepard into space. Yuri Alekseyevich Gagarin orbited Earth once, then reentered the atmosphere. He ejected four miles from Earth's surface and fell to 8,200 feet; then his parachute opened, and he landed safely.

Why Did the Soviet Union Dissolve?

Economics, political pressures, the Cold War, and even well-intentioned reforms all led to the Soviet Union's fall. The Space Race, the nuclear arms race, and the war in Afghanistan drained the USSR's finances. Mikhail Gorbachev, the Soviet Union's last leader, introduced *perestroika* (restructuring) and *glasnost* (openness). He intended these reforms to revitalize the Soviet system. Instead, the USSR's satellite states demanded more independence. The Soviet Union officially dissolved on December 26, 1991.

Conclusion

From Sargon to the Soviet Union, the rise and fall of empires illustrate the cycle of history. What can we learn from the achievements and failures of these remarkable empires? They all had one thing in common: the burning desire to achieve greatness. Ambition propelled empire-builders forward, enabling them to breach barriers and struggle for superiority. Ambition, innovation, and leadership built these empires. Exploitation and the inability to confront internal or external threats destroyed them.

Empire builders had lofty goals. Although they were power-hungry, many brought reforms. Qin Shi Huang of China chose officials based on competence. He investigated and punished corruption and misconduct. The French Revolution, although horrifically bloody, overthrew feudalism. It introduced democratic principles like representative government and freedom of speech.

However, ambition is self-destructive if it leads to exploitation. Achievements gained in this way eventually crumble, as in the Aztec Empire. Suffering under crushing tribute payments and distraught that the Aztecs took their children as sacrifices to their bloodthirsty gods, the tribes the Aztecs conquered allied with the Spaniards to destroy the empire. Likewise, exploitation led to uprisings in the British Empire's American, Asian, and African colonies. It was too difficult to maintain control of vast territories with rebellious people.

Empires also failed when they strayed from their foundations. The Roman Republic, built on a semi-democratic system of checks and balances, persisted for almost five centuries. It imploded due to the increasing corruption of its senators, who overlooked the needs of the ordinary people, like the soldiers who had been fighting for decades, expanding the empire.

Empire builders like Sargon the Great, Ptolemy I, and Genghis Khan were powerful enough to build empires that lasted 150 years or longer. Their descendants grew their empires through several generations. Sargon and Genghis ruthlessly squelched rebellions, as their successors did. On the other hand, Ptolemy forged a friendship with the Egyptians by respecting their culture, restoring their temples, and honoring their gods. He set the stage for a three-century empire. It ultimately crumbled through the intrigue and weak leadership of the inbred Ptolemy family, leaving them wide open to Rome's ambitions.

Though at times corrupt and destructive, empires came with benefits. Cultural exchange led to tremendous advancements. As people shared ideas, they surged ahead in knowledge, technology, and innovation. Empires enabled large military forces. They could enlarge the empire through invasions and deflect attacks from other countries. The Akkadian Empire and Roman Republic achieved remarkable infrastructure such as postal systems and excellent roads. The relative peace of empires led to lucrative trade. The systems put in place by our world's empires still impact us today.

Here's another book by Enthralling History that you might like

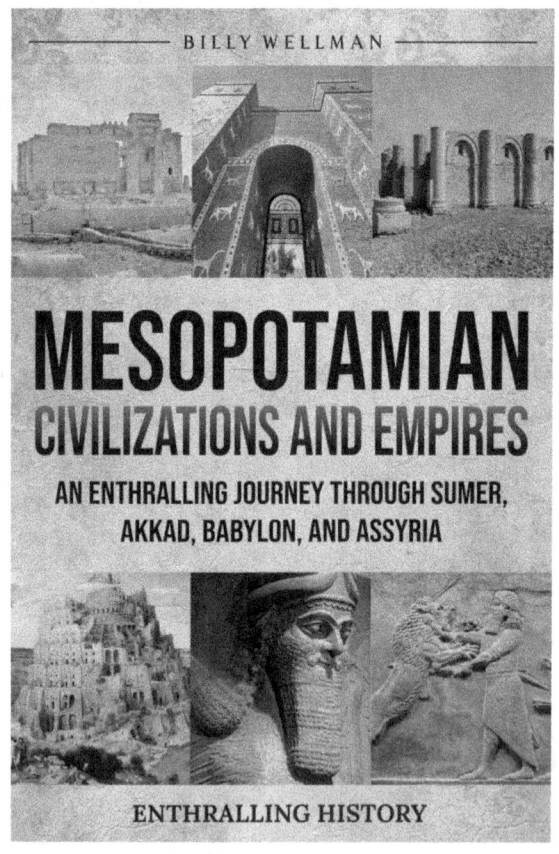

Free limited time bonus

Stop for a moment. We have a free bonus set up for you. The problem is this: we forget 90% of everything that we read after 7 days. Crazy fact, right? Here's the solution: we've created a printable, 1-page pdf summary for this book that you're reading now. All you have to do to get your free pdf summary is to go to the following website:
https://livetolearn.lpages.co/enthrallinghistory/

Or, Scan the QR code!

Once you do, it will be intuitive. Enjoy, and thank you!

Bibliography

Barchiesi, Alessandro and Walter Scheidel. *The Oxford Handbook of Roman Studies.* Oxford University Press, 2010.

Beate, Dignas and Engelbert Winter. *Rome and Persia in Late Antiquity. Neighbours and Rivals.* Cambridge University Press, 2007.

Bevan, E. R. *The House of Ptolemy.* Methuen Publishing, 1927. https://penelope.uchicago.edu/Thayer/E/Gazetteer/Places/Africa/Egypt/_Texts/BEVHOP/6*.html.

Boatwright, Mary T., Daniel J. Gargola, Noel Lenski, Richard J. A. Talbert. *The Romans: From Village to Empire: A History of Rome from Earliest Times to the End of the Western Empire.* Oxford University Press, November 22, 2011.

Clements, Jonathan. *The First Emperor of China.* Sutton Publishing, 2007.

Coe, Michael D., Javier Urcid, Rex Koontz. *Mexico: From the Olmecs to the Aztecs.* Thames & Hudson, September 17, 2019.

Cooper, Jerrold S. and Wolfgang Heimpel. "The Sumerian Sargon Legend." *Journal of the American Oriental Society* 103, no. 1 (1983): 67–82. https://doi.org/10.2307/601860.

Dalziel, Nigel and John Mackenzie. *The Penguin Historical Atlas of the British Empire.* Penguin Books, 2006.

Davidson, Ian. *The French Revolution.* Pegasus Books, 2017.

De la Bedoyere, Guy. *The Fall of Egypt and the Rise of Rome: A History of the Ptolemies.* Yale University Press, 2024.

Dio, Cassius. *Roman History.* Translated by H. B. Foster. Published in Vol. I of the Loeb Classical Library edition, Macmillan Publishers, 1914. https://penelope.uchicago.edu/Thayer/E/Roman/Texts/Cassius_Dio/1*.html.

Duncan, Michael. *The Storm Before the Storm: The Beginning of the End of the Roman Republic.* Public Affairs, 2017.

Elzey, Wayne. "A Hill on a Land Surrounded by Water: An Aztec Story of Origin and Destiny." *History of Religions,* 31, no. 2 (1991):105-49. http://www.jstor.org/stable/1063021.

Eppihimer, Melissa. "Assembling King and State: The Statues of Manishtushu and the Consolidation of Akkadian Kingship." In *American Journal of Archaeology* 114, no. 3 (2010): 365-80. http://www.jstor.org/stable/25684286.

Fenby, Jonathan. *The Dragon Throne: China's Emperors from the Qin to the Manchu.* Quercus Publishing, Ltd., 2015.

Ferguson, Niall. *Empire: How Britain Made the Modern World.* Penguin Books, 2018.

Foster, Benjamin R. *The Age of Agade: Inventing Empire in Ancient Mesopotamia.* Routledge, 2016.

Gardiner, Sir Alan. *Egypt of the Pharaohs.* Oxford: University Press, 1979.

Grayson, A. K. "The Empire of Sargon of Akkad." *Archiv Für Orientforschung* 25 (1974): 56-64. http://www.jstor.org/stable/41636304.

Hassig, Ross. *Time, History, and Belief in Aztec and Colonial Mexico.* University of Texas Press, 2001.

History and Mythology of the Aztecs: The Codex Chimalpopoca. Translated by John Bierhorst. The University of Arizona Press, 1992.

Hölbl, Günther. *A History of the Ptolemaic Empire.* Translated by Tina Saavedra. Routledge, 2000.

James, Lawrence. *The Rise and Fall of the British Empire.* St. Martin's Press, 1997.

Kenez, Peter. *A History of the Soviet Union from the Beginning to Its Legacy.* Cambridge University Press, 2016.

Lewis, Mark Edward. *The Early Chinese Empires: Qin and Han.* Harvard University Press, 2007.

Livy. *The Rise of Rome: Books One to Five.* Oxford: Oxford University Press, July 1, 2009.

Manning, J. G. *Land and Power in Ptolemaic Egypt.* Cambridge University Press, 2007.

Martin, Thomas R. *Ancient Rome: From Romulus to Justinian.* Yale University Press, September 10, 2013.

McLynn, Frank. *Genghis Khan: His Conquests, His Empire, His Legacy.* Da Capo Press, 2015.

McMeekin, Sean. *The Russian Revolution.* Basic Books, 2017.

Morton, Nicholas. *The Mongol Storm: Making and Breaking Empires in the Medieval Near East.* Basic Books, 2022.

Plutarch. *Fall of the Roman Republic.* London: Penguin Classics, April 25, 2006. https://archive.org/stream/FallOfTheRomanRepublicPlutarch.rOpts/Fall%20OfTheRomanRepublic%20Plutarch.r-opts_djvu.txt.

Pollock, Susan. *Ancient Mesopotamia.* Cambridge University Press, 1999.

Popkin, Jeremy D. *A New World Begins: A History of the French Revolution.* Basic Books, 2019.

Sargon and Ur-Zababa. *The Electronic Text Corpus of Sumerian Literature.* Oxford: Faculty of Oriental Studies, University of Oxford, 2006. https://etcsl.orinst.ox.ac.uk/cgi-bin/etcsl.cgi?text=t.2.1.4#.

Schama, Simon. *Citizens: A Chronicle of the French Revolution.* Vintage Books, 1990.

Sheridan, Paul. "The Sacred Chickens of Rome." *Anecdotes from Antiquity.* November 8, 2015. http://www.anecdotesfromantiquity.net/the-sacred-chickens-of-rome/.

Siani-Davies, Mary. "Ptolemy XII Auletes and the Romans." *Historia: Zeitschrift Für Alte Geschichte* 46, no. 3 (1997): 306–40. http://www.jstor.org/stable/4436474.

Sima Qian, *Shiji, Records of the Grand Scribe.* China Knowledge: An Encyclopaedia on Chinese History and Literature. Accessed March 13, 2025. http://www.chinaknowledge.de/Literature/Historiography/shiji.html.

Sumerian King List. Translated by Jean-Vincent Scheil, Stephen Langdon, and Thorkild Jacobsen. Livius. Accessed March 13, 2025. https://www.livius.org/sources/content/anet/266-the-sumerian-king-list/#Translation

The Legend of Sargon of Akkadê, c. 2300 BCE. Fordham University, Internet Ancient History Sourcebook. Accessed March 13, 2025. https://sourcebooks.fordham.edu/ancient/2300sargon1.asp.

The Secret History of the Mongols. Translated by Christopher Atwood. Penguin Classics, 2023.

Townsend, Richard F. *The Aztecs* (3rd, revised ed.). Thames & Hudson, 2009.

Weatherford, Jack. *Genghis Khan and the Making of the Modern World.* Broadway Books, 2004.

Westenholz, Joan Goodnick. *Legends of the Kings of Akkade: The Texts.* Eisenbrauns, 1997.

Zubok, Vladislav M. *Collapse: The Fall of the Soviet Union.* Yale University Press, 2022.

Image Sources

1 Photo modified: names of modern-day countries and seas added. Credit: Karl Musser, CC BY-SA 2.5 <https://creativecommons.org/licenses/by-sa/2.5>, via Wikimedia Commons; https://commons.wikimedia.org/wiki/File:Tigr-euph.png

2 https://commons.wikimedia.org/wiki/File:Ur_chariot.jpg

3 https://commons.wikimedia.org/wiki/File:Tableta_con_trillo.png

4 Photo Modified: zoomed in. Source: Metropolitan Museum of Art, CC0, via Wikimedia Commons; https://commons.wikimedia.org/wiki/File: Cylinder_seal,ca._18th%E2%80%9317th_century_B.C._Babylonian.jpg

5 https://commons.wikimedia.org/wiki/File:Sargon_of_Akkad_(1936).jpg

6 Map zoomed-in, labels of seas and regions added. Source: Enyavar, CC BY-SA 4.0 <https://creativecommons.org/licenses/by-sa/4.0>, via Wikimedia Commons https://commons.wikimedia.org/wiki/File:Alter_Orient_2500BC.svg#/media/File:Ancient_Near_East_2300BC.svg

7 Jans, G. / Bretschneider, J. 1998: "Wagon and Chariot Representations in the Early Dynastic Glyptic," BY-SA 4.0 <https://creativecommons.org/licenses/by-sa/4.0>, via Wikimedia Commons: https://commons.wikimedia.org/wiki/File:Beydar-1.png

8 Rama, CC BY-SA 2.0 FR <https://creativecommons.org/licenses/by-sa/2.0/fr/deed.en>, via Wikimedia Commons: https://commons.wikimedia.org/wiki/File:Naram-Sin.jpg

9 https://commons.wikimedia.org/wiki/File:QinShiHuang19century.jpg

10 https://commons.wikimedia.org/wiki/File:CheLieShangYang.JPG

11 Philg88, CC BY-SA 3.0 <https://creativecommons.org/licenses/by-sa/3.0>, via Wikimedia Commons: https://commons.wikimedia.org/wiki/File:EN-WarringStatesAll260BCE.jpg

12 Photo zoomed in; Source: Tris T7, CC BY-SA 4.0 <https://creativecommons.org/licenses/by-sa/4.0>, via Wikimedia Commons: https://commons.wikimedia.org/wiki/File:Qin_Shi_Huang_Emperor_by_Trisorn_Triboon_70.jpg

13 Luca Casartelli, CC BY-SA 2.0 <https://creativecommons.org/licenses/by-sa/2.0>, via Wikimedia Commons: https://commons.wikimedia.org/wiki/File:Great_Wall_of_China_in_Beijing_(21006986438).jpg

14 https://commons.wikimedia.org/wiki/File:La_expedici%C3%B3n_de_Xu_Fu,_por_Utagawa_Kuniyoshi.jpg

15 User:airunp, Public domain, via Wikimedia Commons: https://commons.wikimedia.org/wiki/File:Xian_guerreros_terracota_detalle.JPG

16 https://commons.wikimedia.org/wiki/File:Cesare_Maccari._Appius_Claudius_Caecus_in_senate.jpg

17 Mathiasrex, CC BY-SA 3.0 <http://creativecommons.org/licenses/by-sa/3.0/>, via Wikimedia Commons; https://commons.wikimedia.org/wiki/File:Romtrireme.jpg

18 Mary Harrsch, CC BY-SA 4.0 <https://creativecommons.org/licenses/by-sa/4.0>, via Wikimedia Commons: https://commons.wikimedia.org/wiki/File:The_First_Triumvirate_of_the_Roman_Republic_720X480.jpg

19 Labels added. Source: Shuaaa2, CC BY 4.0 <https://creativecommons.org/licenses/by/4.0>, via Wikimedia Commons: https://commons.wikimedia.org/wiki/File:Roman_Republic_-_50_BC.png

20 Photo zoomed in. https://commons.wikimedia.org/wiki/File:Venus_and_Cupid_from_the_House_of_Marcus_Fabius_Rufus_at_Pompeii,_most_likely_a_depiction_of_Cleopatra_VII_(2).jpg

21 Stephencdickson, CC BY-SA 4.0 <https://creativecommons.org/licenses/by-sa/4.0>, via Wikimedia Commons: https://commons.wikimedia.org/wiki/File:Augustus_Caesar.png

22 Igor Merit Santos, CC BY-SA 4.0 <https://creativecommons.org/licenses/by-sa/4.0>, via Wikimedia Commons: https://commons.wikimedia.org/wiki/File:The_Great_Library_of_Alexandria,_O._Von_Corven,_19th_century.jpg

23 Ptolemaic Kingdom III-II century BC - ru.svg: Kaidor (talk · contribs)derivative work: rowanwindwhistler (talk)derivative work: Amphipolis, CC BY-SA 4.0 <https://creativecommons.org/licenses/by-sa/4.0>, via Wikimedia Commons: https://commons.wikimedia.org/wiki/File:Ptolemaic_Kingdom_III-II_century_BC_-_en.svg

24 Scan by NYPL, CC BY-SA 4.0 <https://creativecommons.org/licenses/by-sa/4.0>, via Wikimedia Commons: https://commons.wikimedia.org/wiki/File:Ptolemy_(II)_Philadelphos.jpg

25 Burger, Ludwig, CC BY-SA 2.5 <https://creativecommons.org/licenses/by-sa/2.5>, via Wikimedia Commons: https://commons.wikimedia.org/wiki/File:Coin_of_Ptolemy_V.,_Epiphanes_(1878)_-_TIMEA.jpg

26 Jean-Léon Gérôme, oil on canvas, 1866., CC BY-SA 4.0 <https://creativecommons.org/licenses/by-sa/4.0>, via Wikimedia Commons: https://commons.wikimedia.org/wiki/File:Cleopatra_Before_Caesar.png

27 Daderot, CC0, via Wikimedia Commons: https://commons.wikimedia.org/wiki/File:Cleopatra_VII_statue_fragment,_69-30_BC_-_Royal_Ontario_Museum_-_DSC09761.JPG

28 https://commons.wikimedia.org/wiki/File:Roman_Wall_painting_from_the_House_of_Giuseppe_II,_Pompeii,_1st_century_AD,_death_of_Sophonisba,_but_more_likely_Cleopatra_VII_of_Egypt_consuming_poison.jpg

29 https://commons.wikimedia.org/wiki/File:DiezAlbumsArmedRiders_I.jpg

30 Photo zoomed in. Mongol region circled. Source: Talessman at English Wikipedia, CC BY 3.0 <https://creativecommons.org/licenses/by/3.0>, via Wikimedia Commons: https://commons.wikimedia.org/wiki/File:Asia_1200ad.jpg

31 https://commons.wikimedia.org/wiki/File:YuanEmperorAlbumGenghisPortrait.jpg

32 https://commons.wikimedia.org/wiki/File:Tem%C3%BCjin_proclaimed_as_Genghis_Khan_in_1206_Jami%27_al-tawarikh_manuscript.jpg

33 Canuckguy and many others, CC BY-SA 4.0 <https://creativecommons.org/licenses/by-sa/4.0>, via Wikimedia Commons https://upload.wikimedia.org/wikipedia/commons/thumb/9/9b/Great_Mongol_Empire_map.svg/3100px-Great_Mongol_Empire_map.svg.png

34 https://commons.wikimedia.org/wiki/File:HulaguAndDokuzKathun.JPG

35 https://commons.wikimedia.org/wiki/File:ToltecaChichimeca_Chicomostoc.jpg

36 British Museum, CC BY-SA 4.0 <https://creativecommons.org/licenses/by-sa/4.0>, via Wikimedia Commons; https://commons.wikimedia.org/wiki/File:Double_headed_turquoise_serpentAztecbritish_museum.jpg

37 https://commons.wikimedia.org/wiki/File:Boturini_Codex_(folio_4).JPG

38 Ludovicus Ferdinandus; can have elements by Sodacan and Heralder, Public domain, via Wikimedia Commons: https://commons.wikimedia.org/wiki/File:Escudo_de_la_Rep%C3%BAblica_Central_Mexicana.svg

39 https://commons.wikimedia.org/wiki/File:El_templo_mayor_en_Tenochtitlan.png

40 Map zoomed in. Source: File:Lago de Texcoco-posclásico.png: YavidaxiuFile:Valley of Mexico c.1519-fr.svg: historicair 13:51, 11 September 2007 (UTC)derivative work: Sémhur, CC BY-SA 4.0 <https://creativecommons.org/licenses/by-sa/4.0>, via Wikimedia Commons: https://commons.wikimedia.org/wiki/File:Basin_of_Mexico_1519_map-en.svg

41 Manuel de Corselas, CC BY-SA 3.0 <https://creativecommons.org/licenses/by-sa/3.0>, via Wikimedia Commons: https://commons.wikimedia.org/wiki/File:M%C3%A1scara_de_Tezcatlipoca._British_Museum._MPLC_01.jpg

42 en:User:Ancheta Wis, CC BY-SA 2.5 <https://creativecommons.org/licenses/by-sa/2.5>, via Wikimedia Commons; https://commons.wikimedia.org/wiki/File:Aztec_Sun_Stone_Replica_cropped.jpg

43 Ramirez72, Andersmusician, Vadac, CC BY-SA 2.5 <https://creativecommons.org/licenses/by-sa/2.5>, via Wikimedia Commons: https://commons.wikimedia.org/wiki/File:British_Empire.png

44 Dip Chand (artist), Public domain, via Wikimedia Commons: https://commons.wikimedia.org/wiki/File:Portrait_of_East_India_Company_official.jpg

45 https://commons.wikimedia.org/wiki/File:Sepoy_Mutiny_1857.png

46 https://commons.wikimedia.org/wiki/File:Dore_London.jpg

47 https://commons.wikimedia.org/wiki/File:Amy_Carmichael_with_children2.jpg

48 https://commons.wikimedia.org/wiki/File:Mahatma-Gandhi,_studio,_1931.jpg

49 https://commons.wikimedia.org/wiki/File:Queen_Elizabeth_II_on_her_Coronation_Day_(cropped_2).jpg

50 https://commons.wikimedia.org/wiki/File:Marie-Antoinette,_1775_-_Mus%C3%A9e_Antoine_L%C3%A9cuyer.jpg

51 https://commons.wikimedia.org/wiki/File:Chateau_Versailles_Galerie_des_Glaces.jpg

52 https://commons.wikimedia.org/wiki/File:Anonyme_-_Prise_de_la_Bastille,_le_14_juillet_1789_(P804)_-_P804_-_Mus%C3%A9e_Carnavalet.jpg

53 https://commons.wikimedia.org/wiki/File:Guillotine_(PSF).png

54 https://commons.wikimedia.org/wiki/File:Russian_poster_WWI_009.jpg

55 https://commons.wikimedia.org/wiki/File:Lenin-last-underground,_1917.jpg

56 https://commons.wikimedia.org/wiki/File:Revoluci%C3%B3n-marzo-rusia--russianbolshevik00rossuoft.png

57 Steve Knight from Halstead, United Kingdom, CC BY 2.0 <https://creativecommons.org/licenses/by/2.0>, via Wikimedia Commons: https://commons.wikimedia.org/wiki/File:Long_Live_the_USSR!_Blueprint_for_the_Brotherhood_of_all_Working_Classes_of_all_the_World%27s_Nationalities!_1935_(51724375511).jpg

58 Mos.ru, CC BY 4.0 <https://creativecommons.org/licenses/by/4.0>, via Wikimedia Commons: https://commons.wikimedia.org/wiki/File:Laika_in_1957.jpg

www.ingramcontent.com/pod-product-compliance
Lightning Source LLC
Chambersburg PA
CBHW072105050526
44107CB00099B/519